Maxwell's Suitcase

Maxwell's Suitcase is dedicated to my grandmother,
Malka Bein, who perished in the Shoah,
but not from my memory.

*"Who knows only his generation
remains always a child."*

— Cicero

Contents

Acknowledgements

Many thanks to the Forum Writers for their constructive criticism, to my friends at KSU for their support and encouragement, and to David Weberman, my fellow traveler, for translating the letters that lived in the suitcase.

I am grateful to my dear wife, Liz, for her support and patience throughout the project.

Part I

A Dance with the Past

Chapter 1

A Dance with the Past

I didn't know much about my inheritance, even though it was buried just down the hall from where I slept. My father hid it at the bottom of his closet for forty years in a brown leather suitcase. That suitcase had seen happier days before being relegated to the dark, and it sported the badges of its journey splashed across its lid in yellows, oranges, and blues. When I was ten, those colorful ovals and squares beckoned. But my father's old suitcase was off-limits. Only he could dig it out of that closet. Only he could open it. And only he could take anything from it.

My imagination filled the suitcase I was forbidden to open.

During the forty years my family lived in our Brooklyn apartment, I must have passed that closet ten thousand times. The thick glass doorknob looked like a kaleidoscope without the colors, and in those ten thousand trips, I didn't realize that another time loomed right in front of me. It was in my father's old hats, in his old suits, and in his old ties. In that dark closet, the past mingled with the present. My father's old clothes had been worn by the past. His shoes had walked there.

I called him Maxwell, but my father's name was Max. The alias stemmed from the Beatles song, "Maxwell's Silver Hammer." He was old enough to have been my grandfather, and because he had a full head of silver hair, the name seemed to fit. Beneath hazel eyes and angular cheekbones, a gold crown gleamed when he smiled. I too wanted a golden crown, but I never told him.

I didn't know much about my father, it seemed, even though we had lived together for so long. He didn't talk much about his past and was silent about where he went when he drifted off into a daydream, while sitting right there in front of me. Maybe it was the verboten suitcase that made me think there was something about him I didn't know. I wondered what he had locked up inside.

My father didn't speak much about himself, which was common for men of his generation, and especially common for those who had outrun hitler's nazis.* But occasionally, when he revealed his old pictures, he let us peer behind the curtain. He called them his pictures from home. The more I learned about him, the more surprised I was that the place he called home was Germany.

---

* The words "nazi" and "hitler" are intentionally not capitalized.

4

He kept his old pictures in that suitcase, hidden in his closet in our upstairs apartment. It was the same suitcase he carried on Kristallnacht, when as a young man he fled from Leipzig, Germany. Kristallnacht was the state-sponsored nazi riot against the Jews of Germany in November of 1938. That closet was in the hallway, just twenty feet from our kitchen, where breakfast was served with a juicy helping of the Yiddish Radio Hour.

I remember one morning, waiting with my mother and older brother for my father to take his seat for breakfast at the head of the kitchen table. We didn't start eating without him, and he was in the bathroom, shaving. My father shaved with a five-cent double-edged razor blade and used a shaving brush to make lather. He'd stir the wet brush into the mug filled with a round cake of white soap and paint the foamy froth on his face. Then he would clean the lather from his mouth with a backwards motion of his thumb, like he was zipping his lips.

The radio, a rectangular plastic box with a glowing orange eye, played in the background. A deep voice said, "This is WEVD, 1050 on your radio dial, the station that speaks your language. And now the news." My father took his seat at the table just as the newscaster wished us hearty good morning in Yiddish: "A hartzik goodmorgin."

My father looked at the radio. He wanted to listen to the news, broadcast on the hour, and I could tell from his knitted brow that he wasn't going to be able to hear the program over our chatter. He listened to every word of the Yiddish news as if he trusted those words more than English words.

My father got out of his chair and left the table. He went across the room to put his ear closer to the radio that sat on a counter near the stove, where the frying eggs popped and hissed. Even though I didn't understand the words spoken in the Yiddish broadcast, I listened. Somehow, those words meant something to me. I could recognize their beginnings and endings, and I could pick out the sentences. Some voiced concern, some voiced happiness, and some just reported the news. I liked the sound of the language, a sweet guttural music, like warm chopped liver-pâté to some. My parents called it "mama loshen," the mother tongue.

And after The News came The Music.

By this time, my father had joined us at the table again, as a song came on the radio. My parents said, "Oi, ah Frailich!" and they jumped out of their chairs for the lively dance. My father, who was eating breakfast, pulled out the napkin that had been tucked into his belt and threw it on the table. He motioned for us to get up.

And as if by invisible signal, my mother and my father lifted the kitchen table from its customary place in the middle of the room and set it down against the wall. Quickly they moved the chairs aside. They came together in the middle of the room and began dancing, their shoes inches apart, whirling and twisting across the linoleum floor. The room shook. My feet were tapping to the rhythm, out of control, as if they belonged to another body. My parents put out their hands toward me.

"Come dance. We'll show you how," my mother said. But I was embarrassed. I was ten years old. I didn't know how to dance, so I stood and watched.

The music ended, and my parents were breathless. My mother wiped her forehead with a tissue that she pulled from under a rolled-up sleeve.

"Peter, the story of our Jewish people is in that music," she said.

My father said, "That's klezmer music, Jewish soul music. You'll know I'm dead when you play it for me and I don't get up and dance."

That music held something for me. It said something to me, though I couldn't understand the message. It was hidden. But from that moment, I was addicted to klezmer.

Klezmer music was wild. It dipped and soared and cried and pleaded. Klezmer was sweet, but could stampede like wild horses. It could be drunk and funny, or like lace on a wedding cake. I listened to the riot rushing from a clarinet, cutting the air with a steely ribbon of sound that reminded me of something I never knew.

Chapter 2

The Picture

His memories were black-and-white; his stories were in color. His pictures were crisply focused; his recollections were sometimes blurred. They were glossy but dim, those three-by-five time machines that made past moments true. The stories, polished by repetition, were occasionally forgotten. Some revealed a depth of field, but were accompanied by shallow narrative.

Sometimes my father would invite me into the past. Although it did not seem so far away, I thought it belonged to him. But he knew it was something we shared. He wasn't about to tell me that his blood ran through my veins, and his father's through his. I wish he could have said that. Maybe he thought the meaning would be lost on a child. He often said, "Youth is wasted on the young." Perhaps he did tell me, and I didn't hear because the message was packed in a suitcase or in the notes of an old song. Maybe I had to find out for myself.

Although he rarely spoke of his past, his pictures that lived in the suitcase sometimes poked him. I couldn't imagine why else he'd occasionally say, "Come, I'll show you my pictures from home." I was there in the blink of a shutter.

He'd get down on his hands and knees in front of that closet, reach in to clear a path for his old valise, half-disappear into *then*, and drag it into *now*. The suitcase had lost its handle, so my father had to carry it in his arms, like a baby, before laying it down on his bed. He'd sit between us. When he'd snap open the locks and raise the lid, the rising fragrance of old paper, leather, and something spicy made my tongue tingle, like after eating bananas.

That delicious moment was my signal to rummage. I'd try to get a glimpse inside, but my father didn't want to play. He wanted to get on with the picture show.

He'd reach into his valise and take out an envelope of black-and-white photographs, curled like nesting spoons. And in that instant, he would become a different person, talkative and animated, almost as if he had stepped out of a time machine set for a happier moment.

I wanted to explore in the open box of treasure, so I leaned past him on the bed, and I spied a Morse Code keypad in the suitcase. In my ten-year-old mind, it was the kind that sent secret messages to agents behind enemy lines. I pulled it from the jumble and let it sit in the palm of my hand, where I admired it for a moment before tapping out an imaginary dispatch of my own.

"Where'd you get this?" I asked my father.

"In the army."

"Which army?"

"American," he said, laughing.

"What did you do with it?"

He shrugged.

But later, when he offered me twenty-five dollars to learn Morse Code, I became suspicious. The combination of my father's German accent with his secret suitcase, the Morse Code, and his reticence to talk about himself and his family led me to the only valid conclusion that a ten-year-old boy could have reached. My father was a German spy. And I knew that was something a real spy couldn't discuss, even with his ten-year-old son.

"Hey, what's this?" I remember asking, reaching into the suitcase for something that caught my imagination. It was a little, black leather box. Inside the box was a thin rectangular bar, a slim inch of purple with a white stripe on either end.

"What is it?" I asked

"A sharpshooter's medal. I won that in the army when I was a soldier during the war."

He'd move closer to draw my attention back to the pictures in his hand. I still remember some of them. Usually my father would show me the photo of him as a young boy in knickers, on a cobblestone street, arm-in-arm with another boy.

"Who's the other fellow?" I once asked.

"I don't remember," my father said.

And there was another of my father, probably at about my age, sitting at a table reading a book. Behind him was a little girl in a white blouse with a ribbon in her collar.

"Who's the little girl?"

He shrugged. "I don't remember."

At that time, I didn't know why he couldn't remember some of the people with whom he had stood. Now I know why. They were lost in the war.

My favorite picture was the one of him skiing in the Alps.

"Why were you skiing in a bathing suit?"

"It was summertime and the air was warm, too warm for a jacket, but the snow really burned your behind if you fell down."

I liked that picture because no matter how many times my father showed it to me, he told the same skiing story, always as if he were telling it for the first time. But I didn't stop him. I liked to hear him tell a story. It was so rare to hear him speak more than two or three sentences at a time.

He showed me pictures of himself with his best friend, Alfred, feeding the pigeons at St. Peter's in Rome. Alfred looked as though he had parted his hair with a steel ruler. My father and Alfred had gone to school together in Leipzig, lost track of each other during the war, and somehow had gotten back together in New York City.

I remember digging in the suitcase and pulling at a stack of ragged papers tied up with old shoelaces.

"What are these?"

"Oh, they're nothing." My father shook his head and pushed my hand away from the bound pile of letters. He shut the lid of the case and snapped the locks before I could tug on those strings any more. His gaze was off in the distance.

◆

I'll always remember a particular Sunday afternoon, sitting on the bed with him and his suitcase. The small bedroom was crammed with furniture, which made it seem even smaller. The mirror on the wall looked back at me as my father opened the envelope filled with black-and- white photographs. He showed me the usual ones. We talked about them, but then he held out a picture in front of me that I had never seen. He let the perfectly flat rectangle rest in the palm of his hand, for what seemed like minutes.

I was staring at a woman in a long dress with black sleeves and a fancy hat, posing with one hand on her hip. Her dress reached down to the tops of her polished shoes. She looked confident and proud; someone I wanted to know. Our eyes met, and there was a strength in her gaze. I could see my father's face in hers.

My father turned to me, then to the picture, then to me again. "Do you know who this is?"

I shook my head.

His voice became small and strange. It sounded as if it wasn't even coming from his mouth. The room became uncomfortably close and quiet.

"This is your grandmother," my father said.

I had never heard him say that word. I blurted out, "My *grandmother*? Where is she?"

My father had to turn away.

"She disappeared," he whispered.

I was confused. Even at the age of ten, I knew that a person couldn't disappear, especially your own mother. But I didn't ask, and he didn't go on. He had begun to cry and was putting away the picture. His eyes spoke what his mouth couldn't.

I never again asked about my grandmother. I think it was because that ten-year-old boy sitting on the edge of the bed didn't want to see his father cry.

That moment with my grandmother is stuck in my bones.

Chapter 3

The Writing on the Wall

I had never pushed my father before, but he was in the way. I had to. In that moment he became a stranger, and I just shoved him. I don't know who was more surprised, me or him. Just a few minutes earlier, on the way from the train station, I had seen the writing on the wall.

We lived three blocks from the elevated subway line that ran on a soot-covered trestle, an Erector Set. I sometimes rode this train to and from high school, and that day I lingered on the platform for a moment before the walk home. I liked the view, high above the street, where I could gaze at the jagged Manhattan skyline sticking up in the distance from behind a speckled canvas of Brooklyn rooftops.

I ran down to the street, three flights of metal

stairs worn by generations of heels and soles. I passed the delicatessen window packed with bulging glass jars filled with red pickled peppers and green tomatoes. On the next block stood the bakery, sandwiched between the pork store and the pizza place. Then came the shoemaker's shop, where the fragrances of glue and leather mingled in the air with the sounds of light hammering and opera floating from a wooden radio.

Across the avenue down my street, East 4ᵗʰ, I passed the playground, a schoolyard without the school. It was a hundred yards from the warmth of the kitchen where my parents had danced to the klezmer music. We called it The Park. I didn't realize at the time that parks were usually covered with grass and trees, not asphalt. The neighborhood kids, mostly children of immigrants, some Jewish and some not, lived within walking distance of The Park. It was our social club, and I was a member of this society until I went away to college. I must have joined at the age of eight or ten. I don't remember exactly when my mother opened the kitchen door and let me run down the street on my own.

Behind a silvery chain-link fence were the handball courts, with a high concrete wall running from end to end. That free-standing wall existed only to repel a ball struck by a wooden paddle or a hand, naked or gloved.

That is where I saw it. Graffiti. Graffiti was for subway cars or tough neighborhoods. It didn't belong on my quiet street. Graffiti was the signature of gangs. But here, in my park, for all to see, someone had scrawled, in screaming black, one-foot-high, spray-painted letters: JEWS SUCK.

The words attacked me. I knew in an instant I couldn't live on the same street with them. I would have to duck their punch, their snicker, every day coming and going. I didn't want my parents or my neighbors to see those words. They would have to go.

I ran home, trying not to fumble my armload of schoolbooks into the gutter. I ran up the back stairs two-at-a-time. Inside our apartment, I saw my father sitting at the kitchen table, staring into space. He had a sour look on his face.

"Is it that writing, Pop?" I asked him.

He nodded and smoothed his gray hair with one hand, his eyes downcast.

"How did you know? It reminds me of home, thirty years ago."

"I'll fix it. I'll get some paint and cover it up."

My father jumped up and stationed himself in the doorway. His lips became taut. He shook a finger at me.

"No, don't do that," he said. "Whoever wrote that will find out. They'll beat you up."

"Then I'll call the police."

"They'll beat you up too."

"I don't care. I'm going to."

I couldn't imagine why he was resisting, but in the back of my mind I remembered what his childhood friend, Alfred, had told me. "Your father wasn't always like this. He was different before the war."

So, I didn't say to my father, "How can you let that writing go after living in nazi Germany? Didn't *you* see the writing on the wall?"

That's when I pushed him. I squeaked by and ran down

the steps, leaving him at the top of the landing. He didn't call after me or come running. Deep down, I think he was happy.

I rode my bicycle to the paint store, three blocks away, and bought a can of black spray paint for $1.97.

The man behind the counter said, "What are you going to do with that? Not paint graffiti, I hope. There's a lot of it around these days."

"Nope. I'm going to paint my bicycle," I told him, surprised at how easily the lie just slipped out of my mouth.

He put the can into a paper bag and handed it across the counter. I rode back to the park to smother the angry writing on the wall. I remember the clicking sounds that the float in the paint can made when I shook it that afternoon before suffocating the invading words on the cement wall. It sounded like the paint was in a hurry to get out of the can.

I didn't think I'd have enough paint to cover the scrawl completely in a solid black box, so to save paint, I made other letters and numbers out of the screaming words. I twisted the letter "S" into an "8"; the "U", the "C", and the "J" into "Os". I put the "K" and the "E" into boxes, but I was scared as I sprayed the black paint onto the wall in the daylight for all to see. I felt like *I* was doing something wrong, but proud to do it at the same time. My heart raced. I kept looking over my shoulder because I thought about what my father had said. I was ready to run.

Ten minutes later I threw the empty paint can into the trash and stood across the street from that cement

wall, admiring my handiwork. It was as if I had con-
quered a fear, not of my own, but of my father's, and
slain a bit of ugly history in the coliseum on the corner.

Chapter 4

The Musical Voyage

I journeyed with a roomful of nose-picking, spit-ball-shooting fourth-graders learning to play musical instruments. But I wanted to make my own klezmer music, like I heard on the radio. So, when those eager nine-year-olds chose instruments, I picked the clarinet, the lead in a klezmer band. I could have chosen the trumpet and played some cool jazz, but then things would have been different. I wouldn't have seen the klezmer music seduce my ancestors' memories that flew from the bell of my clarinet like a flock of feathered birds, when the time came for me to play.

My classmates and I practiced reading music and counting out time signatures on the desktops or between clapping hands. Cardboard music stands rested on desks holding our $1.75 music books with the likes of "Yankee Doodle Dandy" or "Hot Cross Buns." I seldom practiced and played poorly when I did, struggling to keep a reed in playing condition.

Maintaining that translucent sliver of wood without breaking it against a tooth or cracking a piece off on the ligature was nearly impossible. I cherished the rare moments between squeaks and squawks when a rounded, clarinet-like tone poured from the bell of the instrument causing me to examine the musical apparatus and my fingering, thinking, *where did that sound come from?*

I rented my clarinet from Sam Ash Music on Quentin Road, not far from school. I remember trying to collect the five-dollar monthly rent from my father. He'd say in a rough voice, not belonging to him, "Come back later" or "I don't have that kind of money" or "I'm busy now." Once, he said to me, "Who do you think I am, Rockefeller?"

Invariably, on the last day of the month he'd relent and extract from his back pocket a shiny wallet, a wallet held together with rubber bands. He'd pull out five wrinkled one-dollar bills and hand them over to me, one at a time. I could almost hear the reclusive bills crying when forced from their shelter into the daylight.

I continued playing in junior high school and participated in the lunch-hour band practice. We gobbled our lunches then joined the musical fray already in progress. For a year I played a rusted, dented, dirty metal clarinet, stained from years of other people's saliva and fingers full of the essence of tuna fish and bologna sandwiches.

I hated that old instrument and desperately wanted a new one, but we didn't have the money. My father, who was not into owning anything that he couldn't pack up and carry at the drop of a hat, who rented the Brooklyn apartment in which we had lived for forty years, decided that the five-dollar-a-month rental was a bad deal.

One day he declared, "I know where we can get you a clarinet."

"My own?"

He nodded.

"Where?"

"I know a pawnshop where they sell musical instruments."

I didn't know what a pawnshop was but soon found out about that dusty mine of treasures. My father dropped me off in front of the store with windows of graffiti-covered plywood and three gold balls suspended above the entrance.

"Run in and tell them your father is parking the car."

Inside, my eyes focused in the low light on a zoo of other people's memories laid out in glass cases. Each item in this endless jumble of dreams possessed a story known only to its owner, or to those with an adolescent's imagination. The treasures were coated with a thin layer of dust that quieted the excitement bursting from each piece, the way snow calms a city street.

"Do you have any clarinets?" my father asked the proprietor.

The man looked me up and down, then turned to my father and pointed. "For him?"

My father nodded and put his hands on my shoulders. "He's my boy."

The proprietor came back a few minutes later with three small cases, which he lined up on the glass counter. I took my mouthpiece from my pocket and wetted the reed in my mouth. Two of the instruments were not playable, but the third clarinet was a beauty. Its higher register was within my reach, the lower, round and mellow.

I fell in love.

"How much?" my father asked the proprietor.

"Fifty bucks."

"For how many?"

I was busy admiring my new dream while my father and the proprietor wrestled over the price. Then, I heard my father say, "Okay, twenty-five. You gotta deal," and they shook hands over the glass counter. Five minutes later we emerged from the store into the sunlight. I was clutching a rectangular case lined with purple velvet. Inside, a black and silver treasure.

I remember holding the clarinet on my lap for the ride home in my father's 1964 white Plymouth with the pushbutton transmission. I must have opened the case ten times to examine my clarinet, running my fingers on the silvery keys and over its silky black body. My father glanced in my direction and smiled.

I figured out how to play klezmer music by listening to records, matching the notes with my clarinet, bar by bar, phrase by phrase. I never counted how many times I had to listen to a melody. It would not surprise me to know that I set the phonograph needle in the same groove five hundred times before learning a new riff. But no matter how many times I played the same melody on my clarinet, each rendition was just as exciting as the first. Though I could not match the twists and turns I heard on the records, when I played, I could feel the gravity of something grander. I just didn't know what it was.

But music can go to places where other things can't.

The notes of my klezmer songs were a blessing in my house, rising like invisible smoke, seeping through every crevice, absorbed by the curtains and the carpets. They found their way into pockets and shoes, under the mattresses and between the pages of books. They enveloped my family in a protective blanket.

♦

I was in my bedroom, trying to figure out a song on a record. I liked the tune "The Heyser Bulgar." I was sitting on the edge of my bed, and my mother came into my room.

"The music reminds me of a story," she said.

I put down my clarinet. My mother was a good storyteller, so I looked forward to hearing what she had to say.

"When I was a girl, my grandfather lived with us," she said. "That was in the 1920s, so he was probably born around 1870. He had a big white beard." She cupped her hand well below her chin, showing me how long his beard was.

"My sisters and I taught him to play cards, and he used to cheat by hiding cards behind his beard. We had fun with him."

She looked away.

"It's too bad you never knew your grandparents. They would have loved you, and you would have loved them."

A pause hung in the air. Neither of us knew what to say.

"Anyway," she continued, "one day I was playing the Victrola. Today you'd call it the record player. We had some old Jewish records in the house, 78s, and I liked to listen to them. I put one on, and my old grandfather came into the room and said to me in Yiddish,

"אַז איז אָן אַלט ליד" *that* is an old song.

"I'm telling you this story because that song I was listening to with my grandfather sounded like the song you were playing on your clarinet."

She nodded firmly and said again, "The history of the Jewish people is in that music."

Chapter 5

Revenge – A Boy's Fantasy

"Did you fight the Germans when you were in the army?" I once asked my father.

He looked at the floor as he shook his head.

"No." He took a breath. "I was stationed near Washington DC during the war, for a while with an engineering unit, then in a medical outfit. Because I spoke German perfectly, I ended up in Fort Meade, a camp for captured German prisoners."

"Captured Germans?'

"They wanted me to hang around the prisoners and listen to their conversations."

"What for?"

"The prisoners were high-ranking German officers. Maybe I'd be able to overhear them say something important that would help our boys fighting in Europe."

"Did you ever hear anything?"

"Sometimes, but it wasn't so easy for me to get close without making them suspicious. I couldn't talk to them. I couldn't let them know I spoke German."

"How did you do it?"

"They brought in a German general, Hans Von Arnim, a Panzer tank commander captured in North Africa. The other fellas crowded around; they wanted to see what a German general looked like. I didn't think he was anything special."

"What did you do?"

"Sometimes we played checkers. His buddies sat nearby and they kibbitzed, but I think Von Arnim knew I was a German because of how I played checkers. We had a certain style of play in Germany."

I wanted more of the story.

"One day I came into Von Arnim's room," my father told me. "He had his back to me and was taking off his Iron Cross."

My father said, in a tongue-in-cheek moment, "I thought he was going to give it to me."

♦

I'm sure my father thought his native German-speaking ability, his sharpshooter's eye, and his hatred for the nazis could have been put to better use during the war, and when the topic came up, I asked again, "Why didn't they let you fight with the army in Europe?"

He said with a sad shrug, "They thought I was a security risk."

But the ten-year-old boy who saw his father crying over the picture of his grandmother wanted justice. He wanted revenge. He had heard some dribs and drabs of conversation in his Brooklyn apartment. His grandmother had died in a gas chamber of a concentration camp, in a place called Belzec, Poland. That ten-year-old boy wanted to give his father the opportunity to avenge the murder, even if it was only in his imagination.

◆

Intelligence reports indicate there is reason to believe that General von Werner and other high-ranking nazi officials are planning to visit a newly constructed concentration camp near the town of Belzec, in southwestern Poland. It is a model camp. The commandant of Belzec, SS Colonel Christian Wirth, is expected to be in attendance to receive his big-shot guests and conduct the tour. The visiting officials want to review the design of the camp for possible duplication elsewhere. The information is reliable and comes from conversations overheard by an American soldier in a POW camp in Ft. Meade, outside Washington DC.

The German officers are coming by train from Berlin and transferring to automobiles at the checkpoint in the town of Belzec. They will continue by car to inspect the camp. The train station at Belzec, just widened to accommodate eight tracks due to the recent increase in human traffic, has been chosen as the site for the attack on the nazi officers.

The US military requests volunteers for the potential suicide mission, and my father signs up. He has flown in small planes before, so a glider couldn't be much different, he thinks.

"Don't worry," they tell him. "It is a lot smoother and quieter ride."

He doesn't care that the engineless plane has only one chance to make a landing in the field a few miles from the rail station. He doesn't care that the only escape route is to be snatched up into the air by a low-flying plane, fitted with an apparatus that will snag his glider and drag it aloft again. They don't tell him that gliders towed behind transports are called flak-bait.

None of the natives looking into the sky that evening near Belzec, Poland, see the glider swoop low. No one hears it in the air, and no one is alerted to the four men dressed as German soldiers arriving at such an unorthodox time in such an inauspicious place.

The moonlight is all the pilot needs to find a bit of level landing area. The small glider, painted to look like a German plane, bumps its way across the field and comes to a halt, undetected. A dog barks in the distance. The air is cool as the soldiers emerge from the small engineless plane and stretch their cramped limbs.

The pilot says, "Max, come with me." He points to the others. "You two men take the other side of the plane."

The four men push the glider to the edge of the clearing, out of plain sight, and position it for the escape snatch at 1400 hours. But, there isn't much time.

The nazi convoy will soon be passing through the checkpoint on the main highway, where the road crosses the rail tracks.

My father checks his watch. He and his companions will need to run some and walk some before reaching the abandoned farm house, a straight shot from the station. The soldiers only need to send a telegraph signal to the main station indicating a clear track, all clear for the train from Berlin to proceed. My father is carrying a telegraph key pad and a switch box. He is able to send the coded message by splicing into the telegraph wires strung overhead.

The military checkpoint will be perfect. Back in Maryland, he could shatter the target on his first shot from a couple hundred yards. He wants to kill SS Colonel Christian Wirth, the commandant of the Belzec concentration camp, the man who murdered his mother.

The entourage arrives by train from Berlin and transfers to automobiles at a siding near the station. When the targets are seated in their big open cars, the snipers fire. The noise of the railroad cars and the ignition of the 12-cylinder automobile engines mask the pop, pop, pop of their rifles.

My father is not a man to gloat, but with smoking rifle in hand he is delighted to have hit his target. SS Colonel Christian Wirth sprawls dead in his open car at a railroad siding near Belzec, Poland.

Chapter 6

A Distant Pull

I remember a day in March. The wind twisted and thrashed in a struggle with the remnants of winter. My father took my brother and me to the beach, Plum Beach off the Belt Parkway in Brooklyn. It was close to our home, a twenty-minute ride in our 1959 Plymouth Belvedere, a blue car with fins like a prehistoric fish.

We drove with the windows rolled up and our jackets zipped against the chill. My father pulled off the highway into the beach parking lot and slowed the car to a crawl, navigating to avoid sinking a wheel into the mud-filled craters dotting the lot. Tattered men smoking cigarettes huddled near a boarded-up shack. I wondered how my father knew about this place.

Seagulls racing the clouds screeched in the gray

sky and dipped down to inspect us. We hurried onto the beach. My father held two kites by their fragile ribs.

The water was polluted. The signs on the posts sticking up from the sand clearly said so. But we didn't go there to swim. The early season and the dirty water assured us we'd have the beach to ourselves, a perfect place to fly our kites. It was the weekend, the only time schoolboys got to breathe the same air as their working fathers, so I was oblivious to the wind and the chill and the stink of the water.

The hard-packed sand was littered with stones, broken seashells, and bottles. I ran ahead, jumping the driftwood, tires, and other unidentifiable junk like it was an obstacle course. When my feet cracked through the crust of the dark sand, a crunchy winter skin unbroken by a new season of scurrying sneakers, the sand poured into my socks, into the spaces between my toes. When I slid into an imaginary second base, my brother dove on top of me. We twisted into a giddy pile, with sandy souvenirs in our pockets and ears.

My brother took me down to the edge of the surf that left a ragged edge of coffee-colored foam on the sand as it retreated to the ocean. We skipped stones on the brackish water. My father, who I thought of as too old to run anymore, pulled up a minute later, out of breath, but still holding the kites.

He wasn't very good at skipping stones. European men of his generation didn't play baseball and consequently didn't develop a throwing arm. If I had realized that then, maybe I wouldn't have been so embarrassed by how awkwardly he threw. Maybe that's why I don't remember us ever playing catch.

The wind blew, and my father helped my brother get his kite into the air. I struggled to hold onto my kite, wrestling my body behind it so it wouldn't blow off down the beach, carrying me with it. But a punching gust ripped a hole in its colorful paper skin, ending my vision of tugging the string against a flapping, dipping diamond, circling the sun in a blue sky. I knew that feeling of being connected, connected by just a thin string to something so far away you could hardly see it. I wanted to feel its pull, telling me it was there.

I didn't recognize it at the time, but the tension on the kite string was like my past; as I got older, the pull got stronger and the string got thicker as it creased a life-line in the palm of my hand. When I was ten, that picture was only of a boy, a kite, and the wind.

Chapter 7

The First Letter

On the third night of Chanukah, December 1993, my brother and I were back in the Brooklyn apartment where we had grown up. On that night, the family traditionally would have lit the menorah, eaten latkes, sung the holiday songs, and played dreidel. But we weren't up for any celebrating. We were there for my mother's funeral, to mourn for her in the Jewish tradition, the week of shiva. We were there to take care of my father, alone after fifty-two years of marriage.

The evening after the funeral, my father, my brother, and I had each staked out our own silent territory within the apartment. I was reading one of my mother's magazines at the kitchen table. My brother was in his old room, at the front of the house. My father was in his bedroom. His door was shut. Then I heard a familiar sound, the scuffing of my father's slippers across the linoleum kitchen floor.

"Tonight is Chanukah. Where is the menorah?" he said.

"Pop, we don't need to light candles tonight."

I put my arms around him. He was wearing a flannel shirt and a sweater that a neighbor had knit for him.

"We can light candles tomorrow," I added.

My father's lips grew taut and thin, maybe from holding back the words he wanted to say. His lips would get like that when he was angry.

"No, tonight," he said. "Get the candles."

We convened at the usual menorah-lighting spot in the kitchen. During Chanukah we covered the top of the washing machine with a square of speckled Formica to make a tabletop. On this makeshift table we placed the candelabra that held the eight candles commemorating the miracle of the holiday.

And so, we half sang, and half cried the prayers and a Chanukah song. We missed my mother terribly. She never sang with us; she couldn't carry a tune, but she was always there, maybe humming a line or two and encouraging us to sing louder, or sometimes making faces, trying to get us to laugh. I thought I could smell her fried latkes and remember how they tasted with applesauce.

The days after the funeral were crowded with sadness, the chill of a New York winter, the apartment filled with flowers, and the unwelcome feel of being a child again in my parent's house. The kitchen table was piled high with cakes and other sweets brought by the army of friends wanting to express their good wishes, or share their thoughts or a favorite story about my mother.

Every day that week we woke early with my father to walk to the synagogue three blocks away to say Kaddish, the prayer for the dead. Some days my father was disoriented first thing in the morning. I remember the men in the synagogue calling to him to recite the prayer.

"Mr. Bein, say Kaddish, say Kaddish."

On the ten-minute walks between home and synagogue we didn't say a word.

But in the air of the apartment hung a question. It hovered like smoke, and I could see it wherever I went in those close rooms we called home. *What will be after these seven days of mourning? What will be with Max?* I lived in Georgia, nearly a thousand miles away from my father, and my brother lived a similar distance away, in Wisconsin. Who would take care of my father? Others saw the question as well.

"Where will Max live?"

"Is Max going to stay here?"

"What have you lined up for your father?"

I could only answer with a shrug. I hadn't thought about it.

One morning my father's sister, my Aunt Sidy, approached me in the kitchen.

"Nu, Peter-le?"

She called me by the German diminutive name, like Sammy or Tommy, as she had done all my life.

"Where will Mox-eh live now?" She pronounced his name the way only his little sister could.

"He wants to live here," I told her. "He's lived in

this house for forty years. He knows all the neighbors. He knows the place so well. He knows all the cracks in the sidewalk."

"But how will he take care of the house? He can't cook and clean and buy food at the market. He'll be so lonely all by himself."

I nodded. "You're right."

"Don't you have space in your house?" she asked.

"Yeah, I guess that might work."

I watched her from across the room as she talked to my father in German. They looked like brother and sister, eighty-three and eighty-one, still upright. The conversation seemed animated. My father was shaking his head. I went over to join in.

"What will I do in Georgia? I don't know anyone there," he said.

"Mox-eh, this is the best deal you're going to get. Go live with Peter-le in Georgia."

"Do any Jewish people live in Georgia?" he asked.

"Yes, plenty," I said. "And you'll be with your grandchildren."

He didn't say no, so we went ahead with the plan.

My father had lived in that Brooklyn apartment since 1954. He had rented it for his family for all those years. Perhaps he wasn't one to invest in something he couldn't put into a suitcase and take with him at a moment's notice.

Getting him to leave was like uprooting an eighty-three-year-old oak tree. Getting him to adjust to living in Georgia was like replanting an eighty-three-year-old oak tree.

But first, my brother and I had to settle into the unpleasant task of separating ourselves from landmarks of our past, the furniture, dishes, tables, and chairs we had grown up with. In a matter of days, we would have to say goodbye to those old silent friends that now seemed to clutter the house and our decisions.

We puzzled over the fancy glasses and silverware my parents had received as wedding presents in 1942. They were gifts from his childhood friend, Alfred, the man whose hair looked like it had been parted with a steel ruler.

We could only take some of his belongings, but I didn't know how to wrap up my mother's stories that we heard every evening at dinner, or the laughter or the smell of her cooking to take with me.

My brother and I packed up my father's favorite clothing, his desk, his easy chair, some books, and a few other things that would go with him to Georgia. He had just lost his soulmate of fifty-two years, and for the first time in memory he wasn't out there directing traffic, telling us what to do. He was quiet. He let his sons take charge.

"Pop, should we take this?" I would hold up a tie or a pair of shoes I hadn't seen him wear in years. He just shrugged, lost in his thoughts.

Then, when I was cleaning out his closet, I saw it. I saw the old suitcase where my grandmother's picture lived. I remembered seeing that picture in my father's hand when I was a boy. The excitement of the suitcase returned. In a second I became ten years old. It was the suitcase I was forbidden to open. It was the suitcase I filled with my imagination. Again, I heard my father's voice grow small and teary as he described the black and white photo years ago.

"This is your grandmother," he had said.

I had to have that old suitcase. Its dark-brown leather was splattered with colored decals announcing the names of hotels in Paris, Venice, and Budapest, places where it had traveled with my father in the 1930s, before its sixty-year stint in the darkness of basements and closets.

I asked my brother if he'd mind if I took the old suitcase. I anticipated the type of negotiation that we had had in the past over sharing chocolate bars and bicycles.

"You can take it, Peter," he said. Evidently it didn't have the same captivating pull on him as it had on me.

The suitcase had always been in my father's possession, physical or psychological, under the invisible cloak of his dominion, off limits to exploration. I knew about the suitcase when I was a boy, because it is where my grandmother's picture lived. But the thought had never crossed my mind to open it on my own, outside of my father's presence.

After the move to Georgia, about a year before my father died, his force field over the suitcase had weakened. Perhaps it had been sapped by the move. By that time, he was in his own apartment nearby, and the suitcase was in my basement. My curiosity began to overpower the feeling that sometimes told me my father was still watching. I felt drawn into the basement and compelled to open the old valise.

I didn't ask him about the suitcase. I didn't call him on the phone. I just had to open it.

I pulled back two little levers on the front of the suitcase that would release the tension in the spring-loaded mechanism of the locks. But what would I do if it was locked and the case didn't open? Would I be able to cut a hole in this precious leather skin? The clasps securing the suitcase popped open. I did think about the old movie, *The Curse of the Mummy,* and how misfortune came to the archaeologists who entered the mummy's tomb. It didn't matter.

I raised the lid.

The first thing that struck me as I opened the suitcase was that special smell, a combination of old leather, old paper, and something with a spicy aroma, something I could never identify. That scent reminded me of the times I spent with my father, looking at his pictures from home.

Inside the suitcase were those stacks of papers bound in old shoelaces I remembered from years before, but when I took a closer look, I saw they were envelopes. I still felt that I was intruding, so I didn't linger or explore. I only took out one envelope and closed the suitcase, like a jewel thief who had triggered the burglar alarm in the museum.

The bluish envelope I held was addressed to Max Bein, care of Philip Hart in Corona, New York, Amerika. The postmark was May 2, 1939. The return address said M. Bein, Gorlice, Poland. I had met Philip Hart. He was my father's cousin, who had posted a $500 bond – a small fortune in those days, and bailed my father out of Ellis

Island in 1938, after he came from Germany. I can imagine that $500 was a small fortune in those days.

A thousand thoughts bombarded me in the time it took to slide the letter out of the envelope. I didn't know how the paper would respond to its first human touch in who-knew-how-long. The letter was handwritten in pencil, on lined paper. The top of the letter was dated April 17, 1939, but the paper looked neat and crisp, as if it had been mailed yesterday. I could only understand a few of the German words, the first three and last three: "My dear Max" and "your loving mother." I didn't need to know more just then. I couldn't have absorbed any more thoughts running through me. I was holding a letter from my lost grandmother. The letter was more than sixty years old.

It was electricity in my hands.

After a sleepless night wrestling with my imagination over the contents of the letter, I went into the office. I worked in the data processing department of a textile mill, about fifteen minutes from my house. I was completely unable to concentrate. My brain was in 1939 Poland. I couldn't hear my coworkers' conversations about Auburn football, or the upcoming Tennessee game. They were in another world.

Luckily, we had none of the typical technological emergencies that day, so I left early and drove straight to my father's apartment, a short distance away. I was looking forward to talking to him about the letter. I was looking forward to appeasing my racing imagination.

I knocked on his door, but there was no answer. When

I turned the knob, the door opened, and I let myself in. My father was sitting at his desk, in the same chair, near the same bookshelves, with the same books, under the same painting that had lived in our Brooklyn apartment. The familiar furnishings made the place look almost like home.

I gave my father a hug and pinched his cheek. He took off his glasses and turned towards me. He looked at his watch.

"What are you doing here so early? You never come this time."

His thinning silver hair looked more silver and thinner in the short time since my mother had died. It was parted with the black plastic fifteen-cent drugstore comb he always carried in his shirt pocket, and he always wore a shirt with a pocket. The comb sat behind his eyeglass case under his button-down gray sweater, whose elbows had been patched more than once by my mother.

"Pop, I'd like you to read something for me," I said.

He shrugged his shoulders. "What do you want?"

"I'd like you to read a letter for me."

"A what?"

I said it louder this time, "I'd like you to read a letter for me."

"Can't you read it?" he asked.

"Pop, it's in German."

"It's what?"

"IT'S IN GERMAN."

I was shouting. Later, I wondered what the people in the next apartment had thought of my yelling at their new neighbor.

My father nodded. "Okay," he said, and he put out his hand.

I had the letter between pages of a book for safe-keeping, and I gave it to him. He fumbled for his reading glasses as he made his way to his armchair in front of the window. He sat down heavily and put on his glasses with the thick, black frames. He tilted the envelope into the better light in front of the window and leaned forward for a closer look. It seemed as if he still couldn't read it. He got up, went into the kitchen and flipped on the light switch to the oversized bulb beneath the glass chandelier. Its panels were shaped like flower petals, pointed at the bottom, giving the chandelier the look of a large inverted flower.

My father sat down at the kitchen table and stared at the letter through the lenses that magnified his past. I came and sat with him across the table. With trembling hands, he withdrew the letter from the envelope and unfolded it. He held the envelope in one hand and the letter in the other. He looked at me, then at the letter. He started to read. I saw his lips moving. Maybe he had read ten words. Then he stopped. His face looked as if he had just drunk sour milk. He put the letter together with the envelope and pushed them across the table to me.

"Take this letter away; I never want to see these again."

He didn't sound angry, he didn't cry, but, as my mother might have said at that moment, "Moses, Mohammed, and Jesus couldn't have made him read that letter."

He took off his glasses, got up and went back to his desk.

I was slumped in the chair, gazing at the wall. These were the same chairs and table that had sat in our kitchen in Brooklyn for forty years. My wooden friends were no help. I felt like an elephant was sitting on me. I don't know how long my father and I sat alone together. There was nothing I knew to say.

My father had functioned all these years, not bleeding to death with the dagger of his past in his heart. His mother had been killed during the war. He had survived physically intact, but he didn't go back, he couldn't go back, and I had just made an unannounced, unwelcome, naïve thrust into a tender spot in his delicate soul.

In retrospect, I wonder if I had completely fumbled my last opportunity to have a dialogue with my father about the letters in the suitcase, about our lost family, and specifically about my grandmother. The more I think about it, the more I could kick myself for not having been more thoughtful about the situation.

The suitcase, I would find, was the keyhole to my past. It would connect me to my lost family I assumed had been wiped out in the war. It was one of the links to my inheritance. My silent father was the other.

I understand how difficult it was for him to talk about his past, especially the days and weeks leading up to his escape from nazi Germany, when he had to leave everyone behind and run for his life. Sometimes I wonder if he knew all along I would come across the letters and the pictures in the suitcase and be able to unravel the story that he had been unable to tell.

When I stood up from the table, letter in hand, I hit my head on the bottom of the pointed glass chandelier. I thought I was going to pass out. It was a reminder for me to use my head more thoughtfully.

During the next week, I couldn't get the image out of my mind of my father pushing that letter in the blue envelope across the table. My imagination was back in 1939 Poland, and I wanted to talk to someone who knew about the letters.

I was driving to work with the radio on, and a song that sounded like a klezmer melody came on the air. I thought about what my mother used to say when she heard a klezmer tune: "The history of our Jewish people is in that music."

At that moment I was gripped by the impulse to play my clarinet and the klezmer music. I hadn't been able to play at home in a while because I had three young children, and three bath-times, three story times, and three early bedtimes were my happy priority back then.

I don't know how the idea came to me, but I thought about using the synagogue as a practice space during my lunch hour. The synagogue was not far from my office. It did sound a bit crazy to me, and I was a little surprised when the rabbi said, "Just call me before you want to come over. I'll unlock the door for you."

Outside the house I rarely played my clarinet, the one my father had bought for me in the Brooklyn pawnshop for twenty-five dollars. The case was scrawled in a child's script, my name and address in black Magic Marker.

I drove my clarinet to the synagogue at noon. The

parking lot looked strangely empty, except for the rabbi's little gray Toyota, parked in his reserved spot. I was accustomed to the larger turnout of Saturday mornings. I took my clarinet, and we walked up the steps. The tall heavy, wooden door was unlocked as promised. I gave it a yank and stepped inside. The door squeaked closed behind me, darkening the hallway with the tiled floor that led to the main sanctuary. I passed through another set of doors, dark wood panels two-thirds of the way up, with stained glass above.

The empty synagogue was eerie, too silent. The wooden floor creaked as I walked up the center aisle towards the podium, carpeted in purple. I sat down on the podium in front of the ark that held the scrolls of the Torah. Sunlight streaming through the stained-glass windows high up on the walls brightened the room. The wooden pews, smoothed by years of hands and behinds, sat and waited. They had heard many pronouncements from this location.

It was my lunch hour, so I just had time to play a scale or two to warm up. My favorite melody was the "Heyser Bulgar," the one that sounded like the tune my great-grandfather had called "an old song" when he heard it on a 78 in the 1920s.

I began to play. The acoustics in the space that easily accommodated two hundred people were so different from the sound in my basement. I stopped playing and listened to the last notes as they danced back to me from the distant space behind the bright brass rail guarding the balcony. I began to play again. I closed my eyes and played as loudly as I could. The music came from inside of me.

And then I was not alone.

There was some movement in the last rows of the sanctuary. People were filling those rows, or at least I thought they were people. They did not cast shadows as they moved slowly into the sanctuary and silently sat down. They carried themselves unwillingly, as if obligated to be there, their heads were bent, each covered with the same green-gray tattered cloth. Their bodies had no color, rather they were all gray. They had no faces. I didn't know who they were, or why they had come, but for some reason I thought they were prisoners. There was one who had brought the others, and to that one I felt a connection. I was comfortable in their presence and felt obligated to play for them.

I heard the door squeak and I stopped playing. There was no one in the back row now, but there was the rabbi, standing at the end of the main aisle across the room wearing a yarmulke and a smile.

"I was going out for lunch and I heard you playing. I didn't know you played klezmer," he said.

I nodded and waved to him. I couldn't talk through the lump in my throat. He waved back and walked out the door.

I didn't tell the Auburn fans or the Tennessee fans at work about the gray people I had just seen at the synagogue. But I did take that letter my father had pushed across the kitchen table and replaced it in the suitcase, where it stayed with the other letters for many more years, undisturbed.

Chapter 8

The Ring

It was a warm spring day in 1996 when the nurse called.

"Your father isn't going to live much longer," Peggy said. My brother and I rushed to the hospital where my father had been for the last two weeks, bedridden with an undiagnosed illness.

Peggy was one of my father's companions who helped care for him. Four women, retired nurses, divided the daytime hours to keep him company in his apartment. They played cards with him, did his laundry, made sure he took his medicine, took him shopping, helped him dress in the morning, and put him to bed at night. He called them all Peggy, but it was the real Peggy who I met in the hospital that afternoon. She was standing in the doorway as if she were guarding the entrance to his room.

When she handed me the little package, about as big as a large marble wrapped in tissue, I knew what it was. She didn't need to tell me. I stuffed the ball of tissue into my pocket.

My father had been stricken with a mysterious illness that took away his ability to speak. He could move his mouth and sounds would come out, but they were gibberish. His words had beginnings and endings, they were bundled in sentences, sometimes punctuated with hand motions, reinforced with an occasional raised eyebrow, but unfortunately unintelligible.

When we entered the room, the hospital's nurse was already standing over my father. His breathing was becoming rapid and labored.

"Not much we can do now," the nurse said. "Pneumonia, the poor man's angel."

I touched the side of his face with the back of my hand.

"Why is he so cold?"

"His body is shutting down. He'll be gone in a few hours," the nurse replied.

The words came out of her mouth like she was reporting the time of day, but to me it was like a punch in the stomach. *What do you mean he'll be gone in a few hours? Can't you do anything about it?*

My father's eyes were shut. His arms were thin. The skin was loose and wrinkled and bore black and blue marks from intravenous needles and blood tests. He looked as if he was asleep, but his face was gaunt and pale. He appeared deep in thought, concentrating.

The end of his life was near, after eighty-five

years, and now was the time to have that final heart to heart conversation you see in the movies when mysteries are revealed, secrets are shared, apologies are made, and forgiveness is granted. But that conversation was impossible.

I stared down at my father. I thought about all those memories stored up in his brain, which were soon to be erased by a final breath. One moment all the richness of life remembered, the next moment, gone. When an old person dies, a library closes its doors, but it wasn't fair that his treasury of experiences couldn't be saved. There was so much about him and his past I wanted to know. And I wanted to know it all *now*.

I looked around his hospital room. There was Peggy sitting in the corner. When she patted the seat next to hers, I went over and sat down. My brother pulled up a chair next to my father's bed.

I couldn't speak; I didn't know what to say. Peggy fumbled around in her pocketbook, and I couldn't imagine what she was looking for. Her hand emerged with a pack of gum.

"Want some?"

I wasn't a gum chewer, but I took a piece anyway. I was nervous, and it gave me something to do.

She began to tell me a story to break the silence and the tension. Peggy had been a nurse in the Army. While stationed in Germany, she made many friends during her stint almost forty years earlier. Unfortunately, she had lost contact with all her companions over the years.

She said that just a few months earlier, while waiting for my father to get ready for the day, she was looking at a monthly magazine from Ft. Benning, a nearby army base whose PX she sometimes visited. A classified ad caught her attention, not because she wanted the 83 Camaro with 78,000 original miles and new tires, but the name in the ad looked familiar.

"How many Hortence Whiteheads could there be?" she said. "So, I answered the ad, and the address was a PO box right here in town. Well, to make a long story short, not only was this Hortence Whitehead the very same person I knew some forty years ago, but she was living two streets away from me. I couldn't have made up such a story if I wanted to!"

But I had my own story. This is what I told her.

In 1975, after I graduated from college, I worked in an office in New York City as a statistician in a consulting firm. I had been working there for a number of years when a new fellow was hired into my department, to whom I took an immediate liking. I invited him out to lunch. We ate at Chez George on Fifty-Sixth Street, just west of Fifth Avenue in Manhattan. During the meal he did something peculiar with his silverware as he was eating. It has been so long now that I've even forgotten what he did, but I do remember saying to him, "Larry, my father is the only other person I've ever seen do that, and I understand it to be a German custom at the dinner table."

Larry said, "My father is German. I must have picked it up from him."

"My father is German, too," I told him. "He came to this country in 1938."

Without looking up from the table Larry told me that his father also had come in 1938.

"My father came from Leipzig," I said.

"So did mine."

"My father lived near the zoo."

"So did mine."

"My father went to the Jewish school in Leipzig."

"So did mine."

I had known Larry for all of three hours, and not wanting to have my leg pulled any further, I changed the subject. After lunch, as we walked back to the office, Larry said, "Ask your father if he knows the Singer family from Leipzig."

When I got home from work, I raced up the back stairs two at a time, came into the kitchen and went into my father's bedroom. My father was lying down on his bed reading the newspaper. I couldn't see his face behind the paper, just him from the waist down. We had had many conversations from opposite sides of a newspaper before, so I just launched into the story about lunch with Larry. There was no reaction from the other side of the news until I asked, "Do you know the Singer family from Leipzig?"

"Fritz, Hans, or Ludwig?" came his reply, still from behind the paper. "Fritz, Hans, and Ludwig Singer were my friends when I was a boy. I knew their mother and their father. Ludwig lives in New York, Hans lives in London, and Fritz in Australia."

I was stunned. He was not. He didn't even put down the paper. But when my father finally sat up in bed, I knew that something important was coming.

"Remember that favorite gold watch you used to like? The one I kept in the bank vault?"

I nodded. The image of the watch was already in my mind.

♦

Ten-year-old me loved to go to the bank with my father, where he rented a small safe deposit box. After he made his deposits or withdrawals in the lobby at street level, we would go down into the basement vault room, where the safe deposit boxes were kept. We went into the vault whether he needed to or not. *I* always needed to, and he knew I liked the adventure.

Even though my father was a regular at the bank, the guards always had him initial the signature card before admitting him to the vault. This amused him, since he and the guards knew each other by first name, but he still signed the card one more time, so they could match the unintelligible scrawl of his signature on this card with his unintelligible scrawl on the master list. He wrote his name using the old-fashioned German characters that made his name look more like art than spelling.

I loved the process. I felt as if some great secret was going to be revealed. We were protected in the vault by a heavy, black iron gate and the massive round door with all its little timing gears set into the thick stainless steel under the glass casing. Being inside the vault made me think of when Superman couldn't detect the kryptonite stored in the lead-lined vault, or the *Twilight Zone* episode where a bank employee was saved from a nuclear detonation because he was in the vault when the bomb exploded.

The vault room was covered floor to ceiling and wall to wall with hundreds of little shiny stainless steel rectangular doors, some larger, some smaller, each with two keyholes. My father held one key and the bank guard held the other. The dual key process reminded ten-year-old me of the missile launchings in the doomsday war movies.

After the guard unlocked the little metal door, he pulled the long, thin metal box from its chute and handed it to my father. We would take it into a room just large enough for both of us. The room had one chair and a counter on which to rest the box. I always stood. The inside of my father's safe deposit box held mostly old envelopes and papers, but it did contain one treasure that made me beg my father to take me to the bank, whether he needed to go there or not.

The gold pocket watch.

Ritually, my father would take the watch out of its brown leather fitted case and reset the time to ten minutes past the actual time, the way he kept his wristwatch. The watch had usually stopped running between visits, so he'd wind it and put it to my ear to let me hear it tick. He would open the back of the watch to read the German inscription inside. There was something extraordinary about the smooth yellowish-pinkish sheen of the flat gold disk, even to a ten-year-old boy who knew nothing of gold or the watch's story.

My father, sitting beside his newspaper, continued talking. Not a second had passed.

"When I left Germany in 1938 I couldn't take many things with me, and I wanted to bring something that both my mother and father had held in their hands. My mother had given that watch to my father as a wedding present, and at that time it had a long gold chain." He put his fingers together, then pulled his hands apart showing me how long the chain was. "We were afraid to take things like that across the border for fear of being accused of smuggling gold and killed outright by the nazis. I thought the chain might attract attention, so before I left I had it made into a ring with my initials on it.

"Larry Singer's father made that ring."

I reached into my pocket and took out the wad of tissue. I handed it to Peggy.

"This is the ring," I said.

I didn't realize it at the time, but that chain, in a way, was like my past and the tension on my kite string that I flew on the beach when I was ten. As I got older, the string became thicker and the pull became stronger. I didn't realize it at the time, but the chain of my father's gold watch had become longer than anyone could have imagined. It linked me to my grandmother. And in a way, the watch had never stopped ticking, and I was beginning to think it had always ticked inside of me.

◆

My father died that day. My brother and I were standing beside the bed, listening to his raspy breathing. I didn't know what to do. Peggy got up to leave the room.

"I'm going to let you and Michael be with your father," she said.

A moment later my brother said, "We have to let Pop go."

I didn't know what he meant. Then he bent down, his face next to my father's ear, and he told him what a good father he had been, how well he had taken care of us, and that he could go now because we could take care of ourselves.

Then he looked at me and said, "Come back in five minutes. I want to talk to Pop."

I came back five minutes later and had my last words with my father. Between my tears, I could only blabber that I loved him. I had never told my father that I loved him; he had never told me the same.

Part II

Maxwell's Suitcase

Chapter 9

Maxwell's Suitcase

*Suppose you had to leave your home knowing there
would be no return.
You have an hour to pack all that is yours into a
suitcase.
What would you put into that rectangular box?*

*Another pair of shoes,
the squeak of your armchair,
the view from your window,
an aroma from the kitchen,
the cheap string of blue beads
that touched your lover, your mother, your child.*

*What will you need that you can't get where you're
going?*

If only you knew where you were going.

If you fill the box, what will you carry to the next place?
The accumulated weight of your past?
An identity?

And when you've closed the lid and snapped the locks,
you look around to see what you're leaving behind,
for some stranger to pick through with his filthy hands when you're gone.

Would you be thankful to leave with just your life,
unencumbered by a heavy box whose contents you have made so valuable,
you will have to carry them for the rest of your life?

I have the suitcase my father carried around with him for more than sixty years, the one he carried on Kristallnacht, when he fled. He carried it from place to place, setting it down when his arms got too tired from the weight of it all. He hid his past in that box, and he hid the suitcase at the bottom of his closet.

In the winter of 2003 I was between jobs after twenty-five years in the computer field, suffering from an identity crisis because my "self" had been so closely wrapped up in the job I didn't have anymore. I couldn't say who I was. I stuck close to home because I feared some stranger might ask me the dreaded question: "What do you do?"

Aching to be employed again, I wished for the telephone to ring. Perhaps a voice on the other end would introduce himself as long-lost Uncle Bob, who might have had a boarded-up, broken-down hardware store that maybe never made a penny. If I wanted to clean up the cobwebs and put some glass back into the windowpanes, he'd hand me the keys. His children didn't want the store, nobody did, but he'd been working in it for so long he just couldn't let it die.

I would have said, "When can I start?"

But while I paced, waiting for the phone to ring, I must have felt the telltale ticking of my past beneath the floorboards coming up from the basement, from the place where I stored some of my father's old things after he died. I went downstairs to the junk room cluttered with all the what-not we couldn't use, but didn't throw out. There, on top of a brown wooden table that used to sit in my family's Brooklyn apartment, was a cardboard box.

I reached in and picked out my father's shiny metal shoehorn. His feet couldn't have found their way into his shoes without its guidance. The insignia from some shoe store had been worn away, like the ocean smooths a pebble. I held his shaving brush that was still on the string that used to hang from the knob on the mirrored door of the medicine cabinet above the bathroom sink in Brooklyn. I tried on one of his old hats. It didn't fit. I leafed through a 1935 edition of *It Can't Happen Here*, one in a row of books that had been on his desk in Brooklyn for as long as I can remember. I didn't know what to do with these things that I couldn't throw away. They were bathed in my father's presence.

Then I saw it. I saw my father's old suitcase sitting in the corner all by itself. I got goosebumps up and down my arms. It was the same feeling I had when I was a boy and saw the old brown leather case, which can still take the ten-year-old inside me on a wild ride. I don't know what makes the sight of that suitcase so exciting to that boy, who thinks it looks like one a spy might carry, or something Humphrey Bogart might have taken with him to the airport in *Casablanca*.

Maybe my imagination got a charge from the decal on the suitcase from the Hotel Budapest in Venezia, with the silhouette of the gondola. Perhaps it was the yellow oval with the picture of the Hotel Central in Praha, Prague, that made me think of my father's life in Europe and his escape from the nazis.

My excitement at seeing the suitcase bordered on fear. Into a narrow second exploded years of imaginings, and I must have taken a step back before I took one forward, toward the suitcase. I experienced a feeling of freedom mixed with some distress. My father still hovered in the back of my mind even though he had died ten years earlier. I couldn't ask him, even if I had wanted to, and he couldn't answer. Looking back, the first second after seeing the old valise and wanting to open it was almost like misbehaving. The next second, I felt justified with adult reason.

I lifted it off the floor and placed it on the table. "Pop, I'm opening up your suitcase," I said aloud, looking upward.

I popped the clasps and raised the lid.

The suitcase was filled with papers and folders and envelopes of all sizes, and I felt silly that I had waited so long to look inside. The familiar smell of old paper, leather, and something spicy poured out. The aroma took my ten-year-old self back to my house in Brooklyn. I recognized the envelopes holding the pictures that my father had shown me when I was a boy. I pulled a bunch of black-and-whites out of a packet and fanned through them. They were all of the same odd size, small, glossy, and still bent in a slight arc, like a stack of nesting spoons. Then I pulled another bunch of pictures from a larger envelope. When some of the smaller ones fell away, I was left holding a picture of a woman in an ankle-length dress, holding a pair of gloves in one hand, wearing a stylish hat at a rakish angle. She smiled at me, and I remembered my father saying in a small voice, "This is your grandmother."

If electric shocks could be pleasant, I had just gotten one. I don't know how long I stared at the picture, feeling happy and sad and hot and cold all at the same time. I smiled back at my grandmother, and though I had never met her, at that moment I missed her.

I wanted to find her.

The stacks of envelopes bound in old shoelaces seized me. Their ragged edges made them look like bundles of worthless trash piled on the curb. I undid the laces and let the envelopes breathe. They had been pressed together back to back for so long I thought I heard them sigh as I separated them. I examined each envelope. I didn't know what I was looking for, and I didn't know what I would find, but the suspense made my heart and my fingers and my imagination race.

I could see from the postmarks and return addresses that during the war years, my father in New York City had corresponded with his mother, Malka, in Gorlice, Poland, her hometown, and with a woman named Lola in Germany. Also piled in the stack of ink and paper were letters from his sister in England, another sister in France, and countless friends scattered to Cuba, Hong Kong, Buenos Aires, and Shanghai. These letter writers, once members of a close community, had been scattered around the world but still managed to stay in touch. They wrote to my father, and for some reason he preserved their conversations for sixty years.

On the front of each envelope, in my father's unmistakable script, was the date he received the letter. Most envelopes had a second penciled-in date, the date my father responded.

My father had been a stamp collector, so the corners of some of the envelopes had been ripped off, leaving a jagged edge where the linings of the envelopes and the stationary showed through. The jagged edges of those envelopes exposed their colorful insides, letting their pasts bleed out.

The stamps were a jumble of colors and sizes. One envelope had a 40-pfennig maroon stamp with hitler's face on it. *Deutsches Reich* it said. I didn't know why my father left that stamp intact. I thought it would have been the first one torn off. Mutilated. Some envelopes said "Mit Luftpost;" others said "Par Avion." Sometimes one or two postage stamps were enough to pay for passage across the ocean. Other envelopes carried a string of five or six stamps of different colors across their fronts. The slate-colored envelopes were from my grandmother Malka, and the beige envelopes from the woman named Lola.

The letters coming from Poland or Germany were plastered with swastikas and the round seal of the Oberkommando der Wehrmacht, encircling the German Eagle. That seal looked evil. The envelopes were marked *Geöffnet,* meaning they were opened and read by a nazi censor. *Geöffnet* was pasted across the flap of the envelope where the investigator had wormed his way into the letter to do his dirty business. It was bizarre to imagine the nazis delivering mail to the Jews and collecting mail from the same Jews whose bones they burned and ground to dust.

My grandmother's return address on the back of her envelopes was M. Bein, 2 Piekarska, Gorlice, Poland. I got a warm feeling when I saw her name in writing, in her own hand. I took it as a gift from her. Those letters were the only place on the earth where her name still could be seen. I filed that address away in my mind, wildly thinking that someday I might try to find the spot from where the letters had come.

Although I couldn't understand her words hand-written in German, they did communicate a message to me. Somehow, I knew what they meant. When I grasped one of those letters in my hand, I felt a connection to my grandmother. We could share something that we had both touched.

When I held a bundle of my grandmother's letters and closed my eyes I could feel an energy. I knew it was a dream, but I wished I could go to the place where she had lived. I imagined her sitting at her kitchen table, the curtains in her room pulled wide apart to let in the weak winter sun. On the table beside her, my grand-mother has a cup of hot tea that she holds in two hands for warmth when she puts down her pencil to think for a moment. She wonders about my father. When will he get married? When will he have children? When will she hold her grandchildren on her lap?

I wondered what happened to the letters my father wrote to my grandmother. Maybe she saved them in a box and reread them and kept them near to her when she re-sponded. Perhaps she cried when she read them or smiled at a bit of good news. But where did those let-ters in the box go when the Jewish population of Gorlice was marched off to be gassed at Belzec on August 12, 1942?

My grandmother's room was most likely looted by the

locals after the nazis took her that day. They had no interest in a box of letters from Max Bein in New York City. The drunken slobs probably threw the letters on the ground, onto the dirt road outside my grand-mother's apartment at Piekarska 2, and lit them on fire along with her meager belongings—some worn clothes that she couldn't take with her, perhaps a stick of old furniture, a chair, or table. She had no valuables. They had already been confiscated by the nazis in Germany before she was deported in 1938.

I imagine that some of the letters caught fire eas-ily, the edges of the envelopes and inside pages curl-ing black before the orange flame, and my father's wor-ried words carried skyward. Maybe a wind blew a letter from the pile of what looked like odds-and-ends be-fore the flame caught. The wind carried a letter with the name of Malka Bein into the high grass down the road and was picked up by a blonde-haired child with braids who stuffed the envelope written in a foreign language into her pocket. Maybe, she saved that letter from my father. She didn't know if she should try to read the letter that was blown by the wind that day into the high grass.

Perhaps the girl with the blonde braids saw my grandmother on her last day, seventy years earlier. If she was ten at the time, maybe she'd be alive today, and I could meet her in Gorlice. Maybe she would have my father's letter. I knew she would remember my grand-mother and I could ask, "What was she like?"

♦

I opened the envelopes in the suitcase and held the letters close. Some letters were handwritten, and some were typed. Some letters contained messages from two or three people, and the writers used all the empty space on the page. Sometimes they wrote in the margins and down the sides of the pages in different directions, so the readers would have to turn the paper like a wheel to read it all. Some of the letters were written on onionskin paper and sent in thin airmail envelopes. Some were typed on matching stationery. Lola's stationery was beige with a brown lining in her envelopes.

As time passed and the war progressed, the writers first ran out of matching envelopes. Then they used any kind of paper they could get, a half of a torn page or onionskin that became unreadable when inked on both sides with a fountain pen. When Lola's black typewriter ribbon ran out, she typed on the red strip. When that ran out, she wrote by hand.

I was amazed at how well the paper had survived all those years in the suitcase. I could tell by the postmarks that they had all been written between 1938 and 1941. But their stories had been bound inside a dark box, and it was time to let them go free.

While the suitcase held my father's past, I came to realize that it also held mine. It was something we could share, even though my father had already died. We could share that past he couldn't talk about. Maybe he hoped I'd look into the suitcase one day instead of taking it to the garbage dump. Perhaps he hoped I would take an interest in the suitcase and be able to decipher what weighed on him every day, but was too difficult to speak.

Like his past weighed on him, the suitcase became a weight on me. He couldn't get rid of it and neither could I. It became a weight when I had accepted the responsibility of looking after our past, which could be heavy and delicate like Maxwell's suitcase, which was beginning to show its age. The old leather was drying out and the suitcase, not to be forgotten, was leaving its rusty mark on everything it touched.

I never got that call from long-lost Uncle Bob. It came from my father and long-lost grandmother Malka, who left me a gift, my inheritance. Although sometimes I wondered why I ended up with that suitcase. I felt obligated to translate all those letters, to know all the people in the pictures, and to find out who they are, or who they were.

I don't know why I waited so long to open the suitcase again; I guess any earlier wasn't the right time. I had been busy with life—working, traveling, and being a father and a husband. Any earlier, I wouldn't have been ready to uncover the past hidden inside, and I wouldn't have been ready to accept the responsibility for its care.

The suitcase is a museum in a box. My father had been the curator, but he never admitted the public.

Chapter 10

Between Beck and Belotetski

My favorite history exhibit in the museum of my father's suitcase was his Polish passport. Even though he was born in Germany, German citizenship in 1911 was conferred by way of one's mother. My grandmother, who was born in Poland, was a Polish citizen, and therefore so was my father.

Under the dark green cover of the Polska Paszport is my father's picture at about age twenty-five. I am touched by his serious look, his starched collar and tie with a thick knot, his wide forehead, and his jet-black hair. I can see my son's face in his.

In 1938 he intended to go to Czechoslovakia and received a round, blue-inked visa stamp in his passport from the Konsul of Ceskoslovenska in Lipsko, Leipzig in Polish. Above the stamp in big red letters, scrawled with a red crayon, like a red-hot iron brand right in the middle of the page, is the word JID: Jew.

It makes me sad to look at that page, and although I did nothing to survive the wounds gouged by those three red letters, it makes me proud to know that my father's history is also my history. I am here because he survived those awful days.

◆

On the pages of the passenger list of the *Nieuw Amsterdam* that sailed Thursday, December 8, 1938 from Bologne-Sur-Mer in the north of France to New York City, Max Bein appears on page seventeen of the Tourist Class register, between Beck and Belotetski.

The List of Passengers included ads for future voyages:

"Around South America, 46 days, 14 ports, 9 countries, $720 and up."

Rental of a deck chair was $1.50 for the voyage, $1.00 for the cushion. But aside from it being winter on the North Atlantic, I couldn't imagine my father relaxing in a deck chair while his mother, Malka, and his sisters were scattered somewhere in Europe.

My father purchased a roundtrip ticket on the *Nieuw Amsterdam,* but he had no intention of using the return portion of the ticket. He came to America with a visitor's visa and thought he had to play the part by purchasing the round trip.

In his suitcase I found a copy of a letter he sent after the war to the Holland America Lines, the owners of *Nieuw Amsterdam.* My father wanted a refund for the unused portion of the ticket he had bought in 1938. I don't know if he was successful, but he was thrifty, and he did have a sense of humor. I would have liked to discuss that letter with him.

"Pop, weren't you happy enough to have escaped on that boat with your life? Did you really think that twenty years later they'd give you back your money for half a ticket?"

I can see a smile creep into the corners of his mouth, his raised eyebrows, a shrug of his shoulders in a boyish way, his hands held with their palms facing upwards.

"So why not? I can ask, can't I?"

Chapter 11

The Invitation

While I was sorting through the letters, puzzling over the suitcase, a small brown card fell out of the stack I was holding. The card was made of heavy stock, folded into the shape of an envelope, but not glued at the seams like envelopes were. A postage stamp sealed it shut, glued to the flap rather than occupying its customary place in the top right-hand corner above the address. That one small green stamp held it all together.

The envelope looked as if it had never been opened, which was, for some reason, more exciting than discovering an old letter that had been read many times before. My fingers flew around the card as I thought about the best way to get inside. When I went to open the seal for what I thought was the first time; however, I saw the stamp had already been skillfully slit, probably by my father, more than sixty years earlier. The card had been pressed in the stack, tied up with the other letters for so long that the seal still looked smooth and intact.

Although the card was postmarked August 1939, it looked like it had been printed yesterday. It came from Gorlice, my family's hometown, which in 1939 was a town of about 10,000 people, sixty miles southeast of Krakow, in Galicia, southern Poland. The card was sent by Majer Frauwirt, who I now know to be my great uncle, my grandmother's brother.

I thought that my great-uncle Majer must have been well known in town, because the return address on the envelope had no street name or number. It only said "Majer Frauwirt, Gorlice, Poland." Even though I couldn't read the German, when I unfolded the card, I immediately knew what it said.

Zur Trauung von
Ida Frauwirt
mit
Moses Moster
welche Freitag am, 25 August 1939 um 4:30 Nachmittags
in Gorlice stattfinden wird, werden Sie hoflichst eingeladen.
Eltern und Brautpaar

I felt as if I was being invited to the wedding of my cousin, Ida Frauwirt, mit her husband to be, Moses Moster.

Majer's children were the cousins that my father had told me about years before. He was traveling through Poland in 1937, and his train back to Leipzig took him close to Gorlice. He wanted to see his family, but he didn't have enough money to buy them presents, and he didn't want to arrive empty-handed, so he decided not to go. He never saw them after that because of the war. My father was haunted by that incident for the rest of his life.

Now, though, I was cordially invited by the parents and the bridal couple to be present in Gorlice at 4:30 in the afternoon, August 25. My father had not been able to visit his cousins or go to the wedding, so I thought he would be happy for me to go in his place. While I held the invitation, I studied some of the old black-and-white pictures of my family that lived in my father's suitcase. I wanted to be able to recognize family members when I got there.

I closed my eyes and thought about my cousins Ida and Moses in Poland in 1939 on their wedding day. I was a link in a chain. I extended my arms, one hand holding the invitation, the other stretched towards the pictures of my father, my grandmother, and the woman named Lola.

The summer sun still hung above the treetops at four-thirty that Friday afternoon in August. Sabbath would not come to Gorlice for another few hours.

The sky was hazy, the sun weak, as we walked to the

synagogue in a convocation of hats, the crowd enveloped in a soup of Yiddish and Polish and German. Men in black satin coats wore fur hats, great crowns of fur, not against the cold, but as part of their family's religious custom. Young boys wore yarmulkes that stuck to their heads somehow, even as they raced between the more leisurely paced adults. The modernly dressed men wore dark suits and black homburgs with curled brims. The women wore white silken gloves and hats with swooping brims, some with bows and ribbons gathered in intricate pleats and folds forming flowery shapes. Their silk gowns rustled like the fall wind through the leaves.

The synagogue was a two-story building with wide windows, their tops curved in a half-moon shape. Some panes were open to the outside air. The women entered through a separate entrance into the high-ceilinged sanctuary that was adorned with a painting of two lions holding the Ten Commandments. The wedding canopy waited in the courtyard, where, by a corner table in the shade of an overhanging tree, the men were standing in a loose circle, drinking toasts and clapping each other on the back.

"L'chaim, l'chaim," they said as they downed shot glasses of Scotch with one hand, while holding onto their hats with the other. These religious Jews could never be two-fisted drinkers.

On entering the courtyard, I immediately recognized my grandmother. She was seated with her brother Heinrich and his wife and children. I knew him as my great- uncle Henry. Malka smiled like my father. I felt a warm beacon flash between us. There was my grandmother, my poor grandmother. She looked just like the pictures my father had shown me when I was a child. Had he been preparing me for this adventure?

I saw the woman whose name was Lola. I knew her from her photo in the suitcase. She looked forlorn as she sat by herself, picking at a stray thread on the cuff of her sleeve. There was a table set for some of the poorer families in town, as was the tradition at Eastern European Jewish weddings.

Plates of delicacies, made by guests for the wedding couple, were arranged on side tables covered in white linen cloths. I saw noodle pudding with raisins, pudding with cinnamon, mountains of honey cake, and beautifully braided loaves of challah sprinkled with poppy seeds. There were plates of pickled herring covered with rounds of thinly sliced onions, and dishes of chopped herring whose fragrance floated across the open courtyard, a perfumed breeze.

The bride and groom were escorted to the chuppa, the wedding canopy. She circled him seven times, while the mothers-in-law held the train of her dress. The rabbi spoke in Yiddish, and the groom placed the ring on the bride's finger. She displayed it aloft. After the ketubah, the marriage agreement, was read aloud, the groom smashed a glass under his foot. Family and friends called out, "Mazel tov, mazel tov."

During dinner, the klezmer musicians played one of my favorites on clarinet and violin, "The Heyser Bulgar." When I heard the tune, I missed my father. I again heard him say, "If you play me klezmer music and I don't get up to dance, then you'll know I am dead."

I wish he could have been there together with his family. Though he never said it, I can only imagine how much my father must have missed his mother.

Warmth poured through me as I watched my grandmother. I saw my father's face in hers. She was doting on her niece in her beautiful wedding gown. I felt like I was home, silently connected to my lost family, and I ached to hug them all but was terribly sad at the same time, because I knew their fate.

These images burst on me as I read the invitation that fell out of the stack of letters that lived in the suitcase. But my imagination was punctured. September 1, 1939, six days after the groom smashed the glass under his heel, the Germans invaded Poland.

◆

The end of wedding parties can be gloomy. Some guests are drunk. Some have gone. Tables and chairs are askew, wine glasses are tipped over. Some still contain crimson pools of fermented juice or have an arc of lipstick kissing their rims. Bits of food are strewn about the tabletops, once covered in spotless linen. The musicians have played their last wistful songs and are packing up their instruments. The clicks of the clasps on their cases can be heard across the emptying room. Parents soaked in cigarette smoke gather their families for the trip home. A rowdy quietness enters and shoves the last lonely conversation into the street.

After the wedding party, I too wanted to gather up

the bride and groom and their parents, but the only place I could look for them was in Yad V'Shem, Israel's Holocaust memorial museum. I didn't know if I wanted to find them there or if I didn't want to find them there. There was always the possibility they had escaped from the nazis. But I searched Yad V'Shems's database and fortunately, or unfortunately, I did find some of the bridal party. The Pages of Testimony stored online at the museum said that the bride, my cousin Ida Frauwirt, had been a victim of the Holocaust at age twenty-six, along with her mother, my great-aunt Sara, at age forty-five. The testimony said that my great-uncle Majer, the bride's father, who had sent the invitation to the wedding, was murdered in Gorlice at age forty-eight.

These documents had been submitted to Yad V'Shem in 1999 by a Rachel Svirski, born in Gorlice. The papers indicated that Rachel was a niece of my great-aunt and great-uncle, and lived in Israel. Her phone number was listed. I took that as another invitation to meet my past.

If Rachel had known enough detail to submit the Pages of Testimony about our family, then maybe she had known my grandmother. The thought took my breath away. Maybe she had known Malka Bein and could tell me something about her.

I had once wished to be able to talk to someone who knew my grandmother, but had given up any hope. My father was my last chance, and I had fumbled that. Maybe I was going to have another opportunity. I didn't know if Rachel was alive, or how old she would be if she were still alive, but I felt compelled to find her. Coincidentally, a friend of mine was in Israel at the time I discovered Rachel's testimony. I called him and told him my story.

"Arthur, please try to call her for me and ask her if she remembers anything of my family." I would have celebrated any morsel, any anecdote, anything at all about my grandmother. I knew so little about her.

I spent the next hours thinking of what to ask Rachel Svirski. The first question that popped into my head was, "What did my grandmother look like?" But I already knew that answer. I had her picture.

I surprised myself by how long I had to think to be able to put down in writing just what I wanted to know. Did my grandmother worry? Did she know what was going to happen to her? Did she talk about her children? Did she laugh? Did she have a sense of humor? Did she have favorite stories she liked to tell? Did she have enough to eat? Was she cold in the winter? Was she scared? Did she pray?

I paced. My head was in wartime Poland.

Arthur called me the next day.

"I just spoke to her," he said.

I jumped out of my chair. *"Your spoke to her?"*

My head ballooned with possibilities. I thought I would have to jump on a plane and fly to Israel that afternoon and talk to the only person left on the earth who knew my grandmother. I thought that Rachel was probably elderly and might be dying, so I'd need to hurry and pack my bags. I'd take some letters written by my grandmother, and maybe Rachel would recognize some of the people in the envelopes.

Arthur said, "She is seventy-nine years old and doesn't remember much. She lives on a kibbutz with two sisters. She's very nice and wants to be helpful, but doesn't know anything about your grandmother."

I thanked him for making the call. We made some small talk, and I felt myself sinking into a deep hole, pulled down by that ten-year-old inside of me who was frustrated by not being able to get any closer to his grandmother. Maybe Arthur heard the sadness.

"I can call her again if you think of anything else," he said.

This time, I had really missed the last train. I realized that if I wanted to meet my past I would have to do it without the benefit of anyone's firsthand knowledge.

If Rachel was seventy-nine, then in 1939 she would have been about eleven years old. Maybe she didn't remember because she was too young in 1939. But I think she didn't remember because her memory didn't want to go back there anymore, to a childhood in war-time Poland, possibly to a concentration camp.

My father had packed his memories into a suitcase he kept at the bottom of a closet. Although he couldn't openly deal with them, he saved them in a box where I found them. However, it seemed as if the lid on the box to Rachel's memory was sealed.

It made me think that perhaps I too had a closed box of memories. Maybe I once knew more about the story I was trying to uncover, more about my father, more about my family than I could recall, or was willing to recall. Maybe that's how memory is. It's malleable and can be worked into a satisfying shape.

As much as I wanted to know about my grandmother, I felt conflicted about burdening Rachel Svirski with another call to try to spring free a 1939 image. I didn't do it. I just let it be. But I wondered if Rachel had been at the wedding of my cousin Ida in Gorlice on August 25, 1939. I don't recall if I saw her at the party—if she danced. Was that her voice, laughing into the night?

Chapter 12

The Translation

I had a problem.

I craved to know what the letters said, but something was pushing me away. Something told me not to eavesdrop on a conversation that had taken place more than sixty year earlier between my grandmother and my father, even if they were both dead. The letters were not written to me, so why would my father want me to read them after he'd hidden them for so long in his secret suitcase? And when I pushed a letter across the table for him to translate, why did he say: "Take these letters away, I never want to see them again"? Should *I* also not want to see those letters again?

I deliberated.

Maybe it was that ten-year-old inside of me. He

never knew his grandmother, but he wondered: *Why would she mind if I read her letters?*

But if I were to read them, would I stumble on some family history that I didn't want to learn? I didn't know what to do and decided to ask my rabbi to come see the letters and help me solve my dilemma. I resolved to do whatever he advised. No second opinions.

He arrived at my house at the arranged time, wearing his customary white shirt, black suit, black tie, short beard, smile, and of course, a yarmulke. I had never seen him wear anything else – winter, summer, hot, cold, snow, or rain. He was always in uniform.

I directed him down to the basement, where I kept the suitcase, and pointed at the ping-pong table, where the old valise rested.

"So, this is the suitcase you told me about, the one your father carried when he fled Germany on Kristallnacht."

I nodded and opened the lid. The rabbi peered in.

"Where did all these letters come from?"

"During the war, my father wrote to his family. They wrote back, and he saved their letters. I don't know why he kept them."

"Imagine," he said. 'The nazis delivered mail to the Jews."

The rabbi leaned in for a better look. He glanced back over his shoulder, turning his head toward me.

"May I hold one?" he asked.

I nodded. He reached into the suitcase and carefully picked out a letter. He held the slate-blue envelope up to the window for better light. He rubbed his beard.

"Who is M. Bein?" he asked, reading the return address on the envelope.

"My grandmother," I said. "Malka."

He looked in the suitcase and took out another envelope.

"Who is Lola Schwarz?"

"I don't know. She must have been a good friend of my father's. There must be a hundred letters just from her."

"And how many from your grandmother?"

"Maybe thirty or forty."

It looked to me as if a question was forming on his lips, but he didn't say more. He just returned both letters to the suitcase and stared down into the brown leather box. His head began to nod up and down.

"What should I do with them? Should I read them?" I asked. "They weren't written to me."

The rabbi faced me with a concerned expression.

"The lives of anyone who reads these letters will be changed," he said. "If your father carried these letters around for sixty years, then he meant for you to have them. Go find out what they say."

He didn't hesitate for a moment before answering, leading me to think that I had asked him a really stupid question, but at the same time making me see there was no alternative. He didn't stay much longer. I thanked him for the advice. What he said made sense, but I felt it would force me to become a trespasser, going into a place that wasn't mine.

I was going to have to ask a stranger to read the letters and reveal things potentially embarrassing, damaging, or personal to my family-to my father, my grandmother and to who- knew-who-else. I didn't expect to discover the location of the family's hidden treasure chest, but I would have been more at ease with knowing what the letters said before handing them over to a stranger. Of course, if I knew what they said I wouldn't have to give them to someone else to translate. That was the conundrum.

I sat and stared at the suitcase. I wanted to talk to it and ask what it thought about letting a stranger poke around its insides. It would probably be as distressed as I, allowing an outsider into a family discussion. But I had told myself I would do whatever the rabbi said, so I needed to find out what was in those letters.

Now I had another problem. I needed a translator.

The translator couldn't be just anybody. It couldn't be just any German-speaker or, heaven forbid, a Holocaust denier. The sympathetic reader would have to be someone who could meet with me and translate a letter, reading it to me while I sat across the table. I wanted to hear what was in the letters at the same time the translator did-sooner if possible. I wouldn't make copies of the letters and send them off somewhere, possibly lose the order of the pages, risk their safe passage in transit, and then wait patiently for the translation to come back.

He or she would have to be fluent in German but not a translator by profession. I had hundreds of letters and couldn't pay the market rate to convert them from German into English. Also, I didn't want anyone who might know my circle of friends or family to be the translator. What if we came upon something crazy in the letters? I began to think that I could become another censor of these already censored words. I began carrying one of my grandmother's letters with me, hoping that somehow it would attract a translator, like electricity creates a magnetic field.

My letters were a treasure to me, and I would have been devastated if something happened to them. I went to the copy store and began to photocopy them, along with their envelopes, front and back. Then I realized that the inexpensive copy paper might last two years, while the original letters which were already sixty-five years old, looked like they could easily last another hundred.

While I was at the cash register in the copy store, the clerk saw one of the envelopes with the German Eagle stamp. His eyes got huge. "𝕲𝖊𝖔𝖋𝖋𝖓𝖊𝖙 𝕺𝖇𝖊𝖗𝖈𝖔𝖒𝖒𝖆𝖓𝖉𝖔 𝖉𝖊𝖗 𝖂𝖊𝖍𝖗𝖒𝖆𝖈𝖍𝖙," he said.

I don't speak German, but having been within earshot of it for about forty years, I can tell a native speaker from a hacker, and this guy was the real thing. But he certainly didn't look German.

"Do you speak the language?" I asked.

"I'm originally from Ethiopia, but I lived in Germany for twenty years. I used to work as a translator, and I could translate your letters. Are they handwritten or typed?

"Some of each."

I assumed there would be a fee involved, as he had done this professionally in the past. I was earning the wages of the unemployed at the time, and that translated into me having a low budget for the project, which disqualified him.

Perplexed, I weighed the possibility of never knowing what my letters said against having to scratch up some money for a translation. Maybe I'd have to start buying lottery tickets. I chuckled. I had inherited my father's frugality along with his letters.

A few days after the copy store episode, I was relating the story to a new acquaintance, a friend of a friend. David immediately said he'd be happy to do the translating for me.

"Do you speak German?" I asked.

"Fluently."

"Where did you learn?"

"I studied it at school, and then I lived in Germany for eight years."

"But I can't pay you," I said.

"Don't worry about it. I'd like to read them anyway. I'm interested in that period of history. I also lost some family in the Holocaust."

I had found the perfect person.

♦

Tuesday afternoons I was transported to the past by the letters that lived in the suitcase. They were written by my father's family and friends, who were swept across the globe in 1938, to Germany, France, England,

Poland, the United States, Cuba, Argentina, Australia, and Shanghai. These were places that either Jews couldn't get out of, or they were the only places the fleeing Jews could get into.

From those hundreds of letters, I was most interested in translating the ones from my grandmother. I had to know what had happened to Malka, and I had to know what she thought about my father leaving her behind and fleeing Europe after she was deported to Poland in 1938.

I sorted the mail. The slate-blue envelopes were from my grandmother. With one foot in the present and one in the past, I'd take a blue envelope from the suitcase, gently slip it into a Baggie, and place the plastic-wrapped letter between the pages of a book for safe transport. Then I'd put the book into my knapsack that held the other translation gear—pens, paper, a map of Germany, and some pictures of my family that I found in the suitcase. I'd drive to the Aurora Coffee Shop in Little Five Points, in downtown Atlanta, to meet David, where he'd translate the letter for me.

In the Aurora it was not uncommon to see blue or orange spiked hair above five earring studs in one earlobe, or a pierced tongue and a floral tattoo around the neck. The contrast provided by the coffee shop's clientele gave me some relief from the world I experienced while translating my grandmother's letters. I wondered what she would have thought about the woman in the next booth. The skin on the woman's arm looked like the sleeve of a paisley shirt, so different from the tattooed numbers on the arms of survivors who tried to hide the shame.

Malka would have enjoyed the aroma in this coffee shop. She liked coffee. I had found receipts in the suitcase from food packages my father sent her during the war. Coffee was rationed and difficult to get. But she would have held her ears and grimaced at the eclectic selection of music blasting in the shop. I liked the music.

Jimmy Hendrix held onto me as I dove into the past.

At the Aurora, David drank double espressos and smoked cigarettes. Sometimes he rolled his own. I remember our first meeting. I was so careful handing a letter across the table to him, making sure there was no spilled coffee or crumbs of cake that might stain the sixty-year-old paper. When a hot ash from his home-rolled cigarette landed on a precious letter, our newly minted relationship almost ended abruptly. I didn't know if he saw me grimace over the ash, which I swept away before it could do any damage to the stationery or to our friendship.

When I would arrive at the Aurora, he was usually seated at one of the small tables near the window, reading a book or a magazine, wearing blue jeans and a sport jacket. In the summer we sat on the deck beside the parking lot. We would engage in a bit of small talk before having something to drink, and then get down to reading a letter or two, depending on their length.

David translated, and I wrote as quickly as I could. I hung onto every letter of every letter. It was the closest I could get to sitting in my grandmother's kitchen in Gorlice, Poland, as she talked to my father by mail.

I set pictures of my father and Malka beside us on the table in the coffee shop as we worked. I wanted David to see their faces, and I wanted them to see us. They looked so proud as they watched.

Sometimes while translating, David would get stumped by a word, and he'd have to stop. He'd look off into the distance, go back to the letter, and trace the puzzling word in the air with a finger. If he was really at a loss he might take off his glasses. Then he'd have a silent conversation with himself, and give a head-shake or two, then proceed with the pronouncement of the word, converted from German to its closest English equivalent. He never brought a dictionary.

When the translation came easily, I couldn't write as fast as he spoke. I'd have to tell him to slow down, or stop and go back. I'd read my last English phrase to him, and he'd fill in the sentence. He had patience to spare.

"I can tell that your grandmother was not a native German speaker," he said after the first letter.

"How do you know?" I asked.

"Her German isn't very good."

"She was born in Poland, so she probably knew Polish," I said. "But I'd guess that her first language was Yiddish. She probably never had a formal education in German, just kind of picked it up along the way after she moved to Leipzig."

In the letters, my grandmother might mix a Yiddish word or expression with her German. Sometimes the German word was written in Yiddish characters. At times the Yiddish was spelled phonetically in German.

I knew a few Yiddish words, which were often enough to keep the translation going. If not, during the next week, I'd ask the oldest man in my synagogue, a fluent Yiddish speaker, for its meaning.

As David translated, I recorded in a little spiral notebook every name mentioned in the letter. I wanted to cross-reference the names of those who might have been family, so I could research them at a later date. Those writing the letters told of who they saw from home, and who was looking for whom. Malka initially lived with her family, and as I met new uncles, aunts, or cousins, I wrote their names in that little book.

Keeping track of their names drove me crazy. My relatives were called by their Yiddish names, German names, Anglicized names, and familiar names. My great uncle Henry was Heinrich, or Onkel, Uncle, but everyone called him Chaskal. It took me a while to figure out that those four men were the same person. One of Malka's brothers was given a different family name than she. She was born Malka Kalb; her brother, born to the same parents, was Majer Frauwirt and Meyer Frauwirt.

A bit of research told me that depending on where Jews lived in Europe and when they were married, some marriages performed by a rabbi were not recognized by the state. Children of those marriages were deemed illegitimate, so they took their mother's family name. If a civil ceremony was held later, the marriage became legal in the eyes of the state, and the next child took the family name of the father.

Some names in the letters were mentioned only once. I wondered if that family mysteriously disappeared, its history lost forever. In spite of the fact that my grandmother and four of her brothers and sisters, their spouses, and children living in Poland were all presumed to have been killed by the nazis, I was hopeful. I was hopeful that out of all those presumed to be dead, there would be at least one survivor, a seed who began a new tree.

I hoped to meet that seedling.

♦

Over the next weeks and months, we translated letters written between November 1938 and November 1941. Sometimes while reading a letter, I felt as if I were coming uninvited into the middle of a conversation, not knowing what the speaker was talking about, but not being so out of place that the speaker had to change the topic when I arrived.

One week my grandmother wrote from Poland:

My Dear Son:
I just remembered that I should write you earlier for your birthday because the last letter took 19 days. So I want to congratulate you my child on your birthday. I wish you should have health and much happiness and we should enjoy each other together again. Thank you for your last letter......

The next Tuesday we read:
I don't believe any more in going home, the way things look. I hear that the stateless have been arrested, so I am happy that you are there now....

I am sitting here with uncle Yantsche and Selig. [These are my great uncles.] Selig is just sitting around and he can't make a penny from his shop. His family has nothing.

And then:
I moved into my apartment. A room with a betampte kitchen.
[The Yiddish word *betampte* literally means tasty. In this case, it means homey or cozy.]

The next week:
I have received a letter from my aunt. My heart is breaking. No money and they can't get out. I don't know what will happen to those poor people. Misery is everywhere...

Then:
You'll need every penny, so please don't send me stamps. You mentioned that you would like to send me money. You can use it more than I. My dear child, you will enjoy spending it more than I will receiving it.

And then:
I have no opportunity to send you anything, because it is as if I am on an island here. No one comes here or goes from here to you. It is just a good thing that the mail goes back and forth.

The next week:
Don't forget to light a candle to remember the anniversary of Papa's death.

In the spring I may decide to have my picture taken with Lola. If I like it, I'll send you a copy. I have pictures of all my children around me at the table. Passover is coming and I hope you celebrate it in Amerika the way we did at home.

Then:
Otherwise no news. I'm often very tired. Too tired to write about everything. Please write a more detailed letter. Rest up. No one can take this. Dear G-d please save the Jews of the world.

Your mother who wishes you well.

♦

I ached to be in Poland with my family.

My priority in translating the letters was to read my grandmother's first. But I thought David was getting tired of struggling with my grandmother's penmanship and her grammar, and he wanted to read letters from Lola. They offered a different perspective, and in the beginning, they were typed.

One of the letters in the suitcase was a copy of one Lola had written to her mother, November 29, 1938. She says, "I'm writing on a typewriter [and making a carbon copy] so I remember what I'm saying." In part, she continues: "You gave me 350 mark which I unfortunately invested in wedding clothes…"

The woman I thought was my father's girlfriend was actually his fiancée. A sour, heaviness came over me when I realized that not only did my father have to leave his mother behind, he also had to leave his wife-to-be. I don't know how my father carried that guilt without it crushing the life out of him. Maybe that's why he locked the story away in his *verboten* suitcase.

◆

Lola wrote love letters, and I was embarrassed to read them and think of my father with any woman other than my mother. In a letter from Leipzig she wrote that "Pepserin just had lunch. He had dumplings and was stretched out on the couch. He's becoming an old man with gray whiskers."

I was surprised Lola would take up with some man so soon after my father's departure, and that he would have the nerve to lie down on the couch in her house, and that she would have the nerve to write my father about it. For weeks I wondered, who was this Pepserin fellow? Sometime later Lola wrote about Pepserin again.

"I ask Pepserin, where is Max, where is Max.........and all he does is wag his tail."

I enjoyed that sweet treat. A laugh was always welcome, because reading about my lost family week after week was depressing me. But somehow, every Tuesday afternoon I felt compelled to return to what was beginning to feel like the rock pile.

My grandmother wrote one for the time machine:

"I thought about what you wrote me ...about getting married there [in the US], it would be easier for you to stay there. No, the girl here [Lola] doesn't deserve for you to ditch her. Getting married is not a child's game, and I think Lola is the right woman for you. She will work with you, not like an American girl..."

My grandmother was telling my father not to marry the American woman of whom he had been writing. Two years later my father married the American woman, who was my mother.

As we read this letter, a song by the Klezmatics, "An Undoing World," was playing in the Aurora. A verse caught my ear.

"Darling never dream another woman might have been your mother. Some day you may be a refugee."

♦

I would have loved to discuss the letters with their authors. I knew the beginnings of some of their stories from the pictures that my father had shown me so many years before. I knew some endings, and I could frame the puzzle, but I needed to piece together the details inside the edges.

What would the letter writers have said had they not feared the nazi censors? What more would I have known had the censors not trapped my grandmother's words with their dirty fingers? What did those unidentifiable words mean? Were they just sloppily written or were they expressions that David couldn't translate? Perhaps some sentences were coded to defy the censor and known only to sender and receiver.

Lola wrote to my father saying she was going to send him a cake. She said that her mother contributed the flour and the butter, my great-aunt Toni, the eggs. Mrs. Schafer baked it in her gas oven so that it would turn out well. At first it sounded like a sweet idea, but then I wondered how the cake was going to survive the trans-Atlantic crossing, and who was going to deliver it during the war? Those words had another meaning I never figured out.

I felt tormented during the time we translated the letters because I found it so difficult for me to return to the present after being with my family sixty-five years ago. I didn't know what to do after stepping out of the time machine, back into the present. I became a regular at synagogue and began to pray for my family. As I came to learn their names and even minor details of their lives described in ink on paper, they became people again.

I had to mourn their deaths.

As I sank into the world of the letters, stories in the news ceased to be newsworthy. I stopped listening to the radio and reading the morning newspaper. The media reporting had become trivial. Anything called news really wasn't important to me. The news that *was* important came on Tuesday afternoons when I was catapulted into another time.

If my grandmother had survived the war, she would have been sixty-eight years old when I was born, and if she had lived into her old age, I might have known her. But we were getting acquainted through her letters, and the connection between us was getting stronger. I missed her.

In her letters, Malka worried about her children. She was happy for them, she advised them, and she praised them and G-d in the midst of the turmoil. I can imagine that she showed their pictures to her neighbors, like other proud mothers might. She wrote that she felt sick near holiday time, because she was alone and missed her children.

A naked letter, a page without its envelope, was pressed between the others. Its words had been squeezed so long that when I unfolded the paper, halved and quartered and halved again, its creases poked out like ribs.

Gorlice, November 6, 1938, was written across the top margin. Two weeks earlier, my grandmother had been deported to Poland. It was three days before Kristallnacht, and my father was still in their Leipzig apartment. She writes the letter to Dear Max and Dear Lola. I don't know to whom the envelope was addressed. My grandmother writes my father not to pay for the coal in the apartment, she already had. She says, "I don't know if I can come home again...I think within 8 days it will be decided whether I can come." My grandmother's passport had been confiscated and she had filled out an application for an identity card, "so that I shouldn't miss perhaps coming back," she writes.

Then, tucked in the middle of the page, not even on its own line, not even in a new paragraph my grandmother writes:

Dear Max, if you can go and if you must go please don't stay because of me because you could miss the ship...so I wish you much happiness for your trip.

I had always wanted to know what my grandmother thought of my father leaving her, and now I knew. She thought she may be able to return to Leipzig, but told him not stay for her. I might have said the same to my child, but what an impossible situation. I don't even know if my father saw this letter sent from Poland, dated the 6ᵗʰ, before he fled Leipzig on the 10ᵗʰ. Perhaps Lola sent it to him later. Malka's words might have offered some relief to his conscience, but evidently not enough for him to ever be able to talk about his mother, my grandmother.

In the beginning I wanted to read the letters in the hope of finding what my grandmother thought of my father's departure. But this revelation didn't cause me to put the letters aside. I kept reading, and my grandmother's character took on more definition.

The letters that lived in the suitcase were written to my father, except for the couple of sealed envelopes that had been returned by the postal service, unopened. Those, I believed, would contain his thoughts, his angst in ink. One of them was written by my father in New York to his mother in Poland on December 8, 1941, the day of President's Roosevelt's famous speech that began, "Yesterday, December 7, 1941. A date which will live in infamy..."

It was the day following the Japanese invasion of Pearl Harbor, and the day we declared war on Japan and Germany. Mail service was suspended between the United States and its enemies. But it took a declaration of war to break the paper-thin connection between my father and my grandmother. That letter my father wrote on December 8 was returned to him by the US Post Office four months after it was sent. The striped airmail envelope was stamped "SERVICE SUSPENDED RE-TURN TO SENDER" and had a paper tape across the short edge saying, "EXAMINED BY 5551."

I debated opening that sealed letter from my father addressed to his mother. I wondered what he had been thinking during those years. I wondered how he could have written in good faith to his mother and to his fiancée, both of whom he had left behind to perish in the war. How did he say he missed them? Did he say he was sorry for leaving? I would have liked to think that in that sealed envelope he said just the right thing to my grandmother. I didn't want to know otherwise because I didn't understand how my father could have left his mother behind while he fled to safety. I thought of him as kindly and gentle, someone who was fair, someone who could give you good advice, not someone who would run from trouble and abandon his family. I hoped the letters that lived in the suitcase would undo the paradox that tarnished my image of my father.

After much deliberation, I did open that sealed letter. It said:

My Dear Good Mother:

I am very worried because I haven't received any mail from you since August 28, and I don't know why. I answered you on August 28 through Lola and on October 4 and November 3. I wrote directly. Did you receive the money I sent you and the packages? You always write so promptly, I don't know what to think...I think of you so often and that you are alone and I don't know if you have enough to eat. Lola writes infrequently and I don't know why. I did hear from her in early November.

I will write her a letter today. Please write me imme-
diately even if it is only a card. Lola writes that you
don't have any writing paper and couldn't write for
that reason. I am enclosing three sheets... You can
hardly imagine how scared I am. I kiss you 1000 times
and beg you to write me very soon. Please write imme-
diately even if it is only a card. Your son Max.

I had never known my father to be scared.

♦

While I did open that letter sent on Pearl Harbor Day,
another sealed envelope saying "EXAMINED BY 7733 was
also returned. 7733 will remain sealed, and it will be
the letter in which I trust my father says just the right
thing to my grandmother about leaving her behind in
Europe, about how much he loved her, but how he had to
run for his life. That letter, postmarked March 17, 1942
at 10:30 AM in New York City, was "RETURNED TO SENDER
BY CENSOR" on July 8, 1942, all for the cost of a blue,
five-cent James Monroe stamp that stuck from that day
to the upper right-hand corner of the envelope.

One letter came from a Walter Seiler, a lawyer in
Detroit, who was preparing the paperwork for a visa
for my grandmother.

Lola wrote to me last week that I should get a paper
[form] #633 but here in Detroit no one knows anything
about such a paper. If it should be possible to get such
a paper in NY then I would be very grateful for that. In
the hope of hearing from you soon.

Walter Seiler

Unfortunately, that paperwork was not completed in time. I am grieved to think a sheet of paper could have rescued my grandmother.

In a way, my grandmother's death could not have been prevented; we are not immortal. But she didn't have to die in a gas chamber in Belzec, Poland in 1942. Her last breath didn't have to be filled with carbon monoxide pumped from the engine of a truck while she stood with her head shaved, naked, shoulder-to-shoulder with the others. She stood too proudly in her picture for me to be able to accept such an ending to her life; then no marker for a grave, no place for her name and no resting place for her soul.

In the bundle of letters that my father saved was a simple postcard with three handwritten lines from the Red Cross, postmarked September 5, 1946. The note was in tatters, but its letterhead shouted in blood red ink. I took it to David to translate, even though I recognized two words, Lola's name and Auschwitz. It only took him a minute to read the card. Our eyes didn't meet. After a minute of nervous silence, he spoke in a voice quiet and low. "Lola was killed in Auschwitz, August 1942."

We hid our tears from each other.

I thought about how my father must have felt when he received that card just after the war ended. He had been honorably discharged from the army. He had been married for about three years and was living with my mother in an apartment in Brooklyn, N.Y.

I don't have the words to express the darkness that must have surrounded him. He had saved Lola's letters and her memory for his whole life, and his hope for her survival was smashed by a simple postcard from a stranger at the Red Cross. It came in the mail, perhaps between the telephone bill and an advertisement for Macy's. How many times did my father read that postcard? Did he sit on the front steps by himself and stare into space holding the card in his hand? Did he check the message one hundred times, thinking maybe the name was misspelled, and that the death notice referred to someone else?

After that translation, I looked forward to my next destination of the afternoon. My son was playing for his high school basketball team, and I wanted to be there to cheer him on, and to cheer me up. His school played in a league of other faith-based schools. He attended a Jewish school, and that afternoon they were playing the Bears, a parochial school team. The previous year, when they played at the Bears' gym, the home crowd threw pennies on the court during warm-ups. They wanted to see the Jews pick up the money off the floor in keeping with the stereotype of the cheap Jew who will do anything for money.

As I entered the gym I got a rush of adrenalin, having just come inside from the destruction of WWII to a drumbeat and the hooting of cheerleaders. Sixty years of jetlag was erased in the time it took to open a door. I sat down next to Terry, a friend and the mother of a player on my son's team. She was following the saga of my letters.

"You don't look so good," she said.

"I was just in Poland with my grandmother."

"That's right. Today is Tuesday."

Our families had been invited to a party that evening to celebrate the marriage of our rabbi's daughter.

"Will we see you this evening?" she asked.

"I don't think I'm going to be able to come. I don't feel like celebrating after reading those letters."

"Peter, you have to go. Your grandmother would want you to. We won, and they lost."

I had trouble following the players as they ran up and down the court in their white and blue uniforms. Their images were blurred; everything was blurred.

Somehow, I had to get to Poland.

Chapter 13

The Rescue

On Saturday, August 23, 1941, my father slid thirty-nine dollars and forty cents across the marble counter to a clerk at the Postal Telegraph Cable Company at 201 East Eighty-Sixth Street in Manhattan. The clerk wired two hundred zloty to Frau Malka Bein in Gorlice, Poland and handed the turquoise receipt to my father. He put the colorful note into his suitcase, alongside his letters.

When I found that receipt, I flushed with embarrassed. My father leaves my grandmother behind in Europe, he flees to safety, WWII begins, she is destined for the concentration camp, and *all he could do was send her thirty-nine dollars?* I stared down at the paper. Even though I knew of my father's circumstances, I was angry. He was working at the time for thirty-one cents an hour in a shower curtain factory in the Bronx. His visa had expired, and he had to stay one step ahead of the Immigration Service that wanted to deport him but couldn't because of the war. But I wished he could have done more.

Maybe I could help.

The telegraph pulses on that August day ran off from the New York City storefront through the copper wires to the Trans-Atlantic Cable, destined for wartime Poland. They left my father behind, but not my imagination.

I thought about Walter Seiler, the Detroit lawyer who was working on the exit visa for my grandmother. If only my father could have gotten those immigration papers to her in time, before the mail service between the US and nazi-occupied Poland was suspended. Maybe then she could have made her way to the border and to safety.

I wondered what happened to those papers. They weren't in the suitcase. I had opened every envelope and removed every letter...except for one. What if my grandmother's exit visa was in that one envelope I didn't open, the one with the blue, five-cent James Monroe stamp, sent by my father on March 7, 1942? It was the letter that came back July 8, marked RETURN TO SENDER BY CENSOR, Examined by 7733. The letter sat in the main post office on 8th Avenue and 34th Street in Manhattan in the Returned Letter Office for four months before going back to my father's mailing address. Maybe he had already been drafted into the army and was in training in New Jersey and wasn't home when his letter came back. Maybe in 1942 my mother just put it on the stack and forgot about it, and it has been sealed with my grandmother's fate since then.

The ten-year-old inside me recalled that moment years ago when he saw that picture in his father's hand and saw his father crying.

"This is your grandmother," his father had said, in a voice not his own; then the ten-year-old boy asking, "My grandmother? Where is she?"

But now I knew she was living at 2 Pierkarska, Gorlice, Poland. I wasn't going to send my grandmother in Poland her passport and visa in the mail and let those precious papers navigate their own way through the maze of censors. I would have to take them to her myself and put them into her soft hands. I felt responsible for her.

I wondered where I'd find her. I wondered what her apartment looked like, the one she wrote about in the letters, the one with the betampte kitchen. If she wasn't home when I came, maybe I'd look for her in the synagogue or in the market square. Did she receive the two hundred zloty my father sent? I wonder if she'd be ready to go home with me. Could we leave together? I thought of how happy my father would be when my grandmother and I walked through the front door of his apartment together. We'd have a party, a welcome home party for my grandmother.

I don't know how long I stared at her name and address on the turquoise receipt. Then I found myself standing on a muddy street. Small wooden cottages sit on either side of the road, their roofs in an uneven line, like old teeth. The street has no sidewalks or trees. The sky is gray. Water has pooled in the wide tire tracks in the mud. The tracks run the length of the street. My grandmother's apartment is in a small house at the end of the road. I pat my pocket. Her passport is still there.

I walk down the middle of the street. There are no people. A dog follows me. Skin hangs on his bones. A broken shoe in the mud. A torn white shirt. A smashed dish. A book. A memory. A spent scream, quiet, motionless in the dirt. A suitcase sits by itself in the road, waiting for its master.

I come to #2, my grandmother's cottage. It's made of weathered wood. The roof is bent. Broken windows are stuffed with bedding. I hesitate before entering, then step over the splintered front steps up to the porch and pull on a rickety door. It squeaks. I swing it slowly to lessen the squeal. The sun is setting. Inside, the house is cool and dim. A burning candle drips wax onto a wooden table. The candlelight barely finds its way into the corners of the room. I peer around a doorway and cautiously come into a kitchen. A pot is on the stove. Chairs are overturned. A piece of paper lies on a table. It's a letter. "My Dear Good Son," it begins. Beside it, a pencil waits for a hand. A Yiddish newspaper sits folded on a chair. August 13, 1942. I know that day.

I'm too late.

On August 13, 1942, the Nazis surrounded Gorlice and carted off its Jewish population to the Belzec death camp.

Chapter 14

The Anniversary

On the evening of the seventh anniversary of my father's death, I went to synagogue to say Kaddish in his memory. In past years I had felt sad going to the synagogue on that day, but something about this anniversary was different. Maybe it was the letters.

While we were translating them, I was showing up more in synagogue. What else could I do after reading letters from my grandmother, holding the same piece of paper she had held before perishing in a concentration camp?

When my father was alive, he liked to see me dressed in a suit and tie, so on that night, in his honor, I wore a suit I thought he'd like. As I went to synagogue, I felt draped with warmth. His spirit was there with me. To make the experience of going to a religious service with my father complete and accurate, we arrived late for the evening prayer.

"We *still* can't get here on time, Pop," I said aloud.

The congregation filled the rows of the synagogue, and as we sang "Lecha Dodi," the traditional song welcoming the Sabbath, I heard my father's voice singing with us. He liked to sing, and the tune was a Carlebach melody, a favorite of his. A circle of dancers had formed, ringing the men's section, and I thought my father jumped up to join them, each man with an arm on the shoulder of the man in front of him.

The service ended, and the congregation drifted out carrying me along towards the rear of the sanctuary. I found myself standing beside the rabbi as we put our prayer books up on the shelf.

"What's the latest installment?" he asked. Shaking his head, waving his fists, the rabbi said, "I still can't get over the nazis delivering mail to the Jews."

"We read another letter on Tuesday," I told him. "My father's fiancée traveled from Leipzig to Paris to see him off at the train station on December 6, 1938 on his way to Boulogne-sur-Mer in the north of France. That's where his boat to America sailed from. She wrote ahead to the boat from Paris."

"How do you know that?"

"The letter is addressed to my father, 'Passenger on the Nieuw Amsterdam at Boulogne-Sur-Mer.' It's a love letter. She already missed him after a day. He kept the letter."

"What else is going on?"

"My grandmother had three children. Just before the

war, one of my aunts went to Paris, then another to England, and my father to New York. My grandmother was left behind in a shtetl in Poland and killed by the nazis. I can imagine her three children never got over the guilt. They never talked about it. They escaped, but left their dear mother behind. It has always bothered me too."

I was embarrassed to have told the rabbi that bit of family history, and maybe he felt it. He reached into the bookshelf at the rear of the synagogue for a volume of the Chumash, the Old Testament. He turned a few pages, traced a line down the page with his finger, and began reading in Hebrew. I knew I was going to hear something helpful.

"It's Parsha Noach," he said. "The Story of Noah".

The rabbi translated the passage. It was about a journey that Abraham took with his father, Terach. They traveled to Haran, where Terach died at the age of two hundred and twenty-five, more than sixty years after Abraham's departure from Haran.

"Based on various verses, the sages concluded that Abraham left *his* father behind," the rabbi said.

The rabbi's young son burst through the sanctuary door to speak to his father, but I needed to hear the end of the story. I glared at the boy, thinking that my stare would stop him from interrupting.

"Just a minute," the rabbi said to his son, and then he continued. "The Torah couldn't say that Abraham left his father behind, so the story is written a little differently. These kinds of things happened. Your story is similar."

"Can I go ahead now without you?" his young son asked.

"Yes, I'll be home soon for dinner," the rabbi replied.

The crowd had evaporated, leaving only the rabbi and me. I felt relieved after hearing the story about Abraham. I knew that my father's conscience would be relieved as well.

We walked out into the lobby as jagged pink lightning illuminated the dark sky, closely followed by a crash of thunder that shook the building. The hallway lights flickered. In a deep voice, thunder rumbled in the distance. We stood in the hallway, watching the sky.

"I don't know what it is, but translating those letters feels like the right thing. I'm becoming part of something larger."

The rabbi smiled.

"Why am I compelled to translate them? Why do I even have them?" I asked.

"We have been commanded in the Torah to know our father's story, and our father's father's story, answered the rabbi. "Not to minimize the power of your story, but it is similar to hundreds of others I have heard about from the Holocaust."

I nodded.

"The difference is that your story is very personal to you through the letters. This story is the story of the Jewish people for thousands of years, only you have a little more documentation."

Again, lightning lit the sky, followed by a bang of

thunder and more flickering lights. I was glad that the rabbi was witness to the dramatic weather punctuating my story. Who would believe such a Hollywood script?

"You are connecting with your people," the rabbi said.

I would have believed him even without the fireworks. *Very impressive, he must have connections,* I thought.

The storm passed. The rabbi had Sabbath dinner guests, so he excused himself, put on his raincoat, and headed out the door into a light rain. I stood in the drizzle with my father, thinking about what had just happened.

Chapter 15

Renegotiating the Inheritance

In the spring of 2008 a fire bell rang inside my head, and the clanging wouldn't stop, because November 9, 2008 would be the seventieth anniversary of Kristallnacht, the brutal "coming-out" of the nazi party in Germany. The approaching anniversary would mark seventy years to the day after my father fled Leipzig and seventy years and two weeks after my grandmother was deported to Poland.

A thought took hold of me, highjacking my common sense. It was a child's silent shriek. *I have to be at my grandmother's house in Leipzig on Kristallnacht.* There was no logic to it; I just had to be there. I had to be in the same place as my family had been so many years before, that place my father called home. If his house was bombed flat in the war, I wanted to be able to stand in the same place he stood seventy years before. If a highway ran through the space where his house once was, I would stand for a moment on that highway.

In one second I had become possessed. That little seed of an idea sprouted and grew and blossomed. It took over my garden and choked out other thoughts. But my garden was surrounded by a stone wall, a barrier between me and Germany. And the wall was higher than the Berlin Wall. This psychological stumbling-stone had more barbs on its razor wire and more marksmen with trained rifles than its Cold War counterpart. After all, the Berlin Wall had fallen, but my wall had not.

Germany was off limits.

My father had wanted nothing to do with Germany, and somehow, I had inherited that contract, which I now wanted to renegotiate. He had never returned to the country that had spit him out, and I remember him saying, "We dropped the atomic bomb on the wrong country." I understood his bitterness and his reluctance to make peace with the place that had cut a measure of life from him.

My father didn't want me to learn the German language. He wouldn't buy German-made products. I remember he had my mother return a loaf of bread to the neighborhood store when he discovered it was imported from Germany. He made it clear to his teenaged sons, at the time, that although Volkswagens were popular and well-made cars, he'd never buy one and neither would we.

I wrestled with myself and asked others for advice.

But when I aired my crazy idea about going to Leipzig, friends and family said:

"Germany, what are you going to do there?"

"Is there anything to see in Leipzig?"

"That's creepy."

"Germany, yeeech."

"I wouldn't give them one penny."

"Germany?"

"Leipzig, there's nothing there anymore. I've been there."

"Germany? Not me."

"Every stone in Germany is drenched with Jewish blood."

But the fire bell in my brain kept clanging, and despite the objections, I still had to go.

I even tried to imagine what my father might have thought of my crazy idea. Outwardly, he'd resist it. But inside, deep inside, from a place neither of us could reach, I could feel a smile come to his face.

If I were to go, if somehow I could overcome that psychological barrier, I didn't know if I would even have a landmark to visit in Leipzig. I didn't know how much destruction had taken place during the Allied bombings in WWII, or how much the city had changed during the Communist rule of East Germany. But I knew that I could at least find an old map of the city to get me to the right place.

The address of my grandmother's apartment was in one of the letters that lived in the suitcase. I tossed "Uferstrasse 18, Leipzig, Germany" into Google's open window. The response came quickly: no matches found.

My dream deflated. I didn't know what to do. I needed a destination.

A few days later I had another idea. I tried the address the German way, Uferstraße 18, with the double "s", and there on the screen emerged the home page of a software company at that location. My dream was alive again. I had a place to go, even if it was an office. I looked for the address on Google Maps and found a picture taken from a satellite, 150 miles away in space. I zoomed in, and when I zoomed in closer, a rush of memory attacked me. The picture was of a house with a *courtyard.*

Chills ran down my back. I remember asking my father about his best friend, Alfred, the fellow who looked like he parted his hair with a steel ruler.

"Where did you and Alfred live when you were little?"

My father traced the shape of a box with his fingers in the air.

"I lived in a house with a *courtyard.* I could look out my window and see Alfred's window across the way."

◆

I knew nothing about present-day Leipzig, other than the tourist information I had found on the internet, but I wanted a contact in the local community. I sent an email to JewishGen, an international resource for Jewish genealogy, asking for a contact name in Leipzig. I said in the email that I would be traveling there in the fall. A few days later a woman in Berlin replied to my email and told me to send a fax to a Frau

Krenn in Leipzig, saying Frau Krenn didn't speak English well, and didn't use the internet. I wrote a short email to David asking him to translate the message I wanted to send.

Earlier that year, David and I were back at the Aurora Coffee Shop in Little Five Points, Atlanta, where he had translated the letters before moving to Budapest to teach at the university. After he moved we lost track of each other for about five years. Now he was back in the States to visit family.

I remember saying to him, "I have this crazy idea that I need to go to my grandmother's house in Germany on the seventieth anniversary of Kristallnacht. I know it makes no sense, but I just have to go."

He smiled through the smoke of his cigarette.

"If you go, I'll meet you there," he said. "And bring some letters."

I filed it under, "Pieces of Dreams."

On September 9, I sent a fax to Frau Krenn in Leipzig, saying I was coming to commemorate Kristallnacht, and that my family had lived at 18 Uferstrasse. I thought about those who had sent messages in bottles or on the legs of carrier pigeons. Would I ever get an answer?

After checking my email almost hourly for the next three days, I received a reply from Frau Krenn. I jumped out of my chair and cheered.

"My English is not so good," she said. "You may come to visit whenever you'd like."

I felt as if I had discovered buried treasure. My

carrier pigeon had returned. I began scrutinizing flights and air fares.

Frau Krenn told me that she worked in the office of a synagogue in Leipzig. I learned from some research that only one synagogue out of twelve had survived Kristallnacht. I remember my father telling me about that night.

"I was home, and I heard yelling outside," he said. "I smelled smoke. I went to the window, and a man in the street cried out: "The synagogue is on fire, stay inside." My father didn't say much more about that night. Tears were in his eyes. I always wanted to know more about Kristallnacht, but I didn't like to see my father cry. I never asked again.

◆

If I was going to make the trip, I was going to need some time off from work. I needed my boss's approval. I knocked on her door, and she waved me into her office.

"I have a favor to ask, but first I must tell you that I am possessed."

She pointed to the chair. "Oh my, then you had better sit down."

I told her about my father's suitcase and the letters from my grandmother.

"I feel like Richard Dreyfuss, in the movie *Close Encounters*," I said. "He knew he was being pulled someplace, but he didn't know where or why."

"Are you making shapes in your mashed potatoes?" she asked with a smile.

I got my time off and bought a plane ticket to

Germany. I planned to fly to Berlin via Paris, the least expensive route, meet David in Berlin, and then take the train to Leipzig, about an hour away.

My rough itinerary included trying to find my father's house, my grandfather's grave, my father's office, and his high school. His school, one of the two yeshivas in 1920s Germany, was now the Leipzig School for the Deaf, according to an internet source. My father had spoken often about the zoo, which must have been near his house; I thought I might try to visit it as well. But I would be happy just to be able to stand in the same place as he had, so many years earlier. Those places had to be there, even if today they were called by different names.

I had to bring some things back with me. My father wore a gold ring with a blue stone; I never saw him without it, and I wanted to wear it to Leipzig in his honor. His mother had given him a trinket that I found in the suitcase, two carved wooden cats held together by a thin string. I would bring them home, together with a few letters from my grandmother. As a boy I collected coins and was intrigued by the notion that some famous person might have held that old penny or nickel in his or her hand. I bought a few "1938" pennies in a coin store, fascinated by the possibility that a family member might have held one when it was bright and shiny. I'd carry them in my pocket. I felt as if I were casting out a net, but not quite sure of what I might catch.

I hoped for a spirit.

But at the top of my list of dreams was to play klezmer

wedding music for my grandmother on the pawnshop clarinet my father had bought me so many years earlier. She had missed so many family weddings, especially those weddings of her own children. But, if I brought my clarinet, I would have to figure out how to get inside my grandmother's apartment on Kristallnacht, so I could play for her. I thought about standing out on the street in front of her house and playing the clarinet, but I didn't want to end up in a German jail on that nightmarish anniversary. The thought froze my blood.

Chapter 16

The Ties That Bind

I wanted to take one of my father's ties back to Leipzig.

His old ties hung in the closet where the suitcase lived; probably every tie he'd ever bought hung in that closet. Some were as wide as a hand; some were as thin as two fingers. They hung together on a wooden tie rack that was nailed inside the closet door.

His ties were all colors and patterns, stripes, horizontal, vertical, some dotted, some shiny, some dull, and some silk. Some ties went to work with him. The darker ones went to weddings and funerals. The ties were looped over long wooden dowels, like fingers that stretched almost the width of the door. The fingers held together as if they were hiding something.

In the 1960s schoolboys wore ties, and my father let

me borrow whichever of his ties I wanted, except for one. That one hung by itself at the end of the rack. It was a black tie with red and green and yellow shapes. On it was embroidered, *Paris, 1937.*

"Pop, can I wear that one?"

"Here take this other one," he said. "It's newer. It looks nicer."

"How did you get a tie from the 1937 Paris World's Fair?"

"Someday when you're older I'll tell you."

He never told me.

I wish he hadn't left it to me to figure out. But that was the tie I never got to wear, and the one I wanted to take with me to Leipzig. Unfortunately, I didn't think to take it with me when my father moved out of the old apartment.

I figured out its story after finding a picture in the suitcase of my grandmother, her graying, wiry hair pulled back, looking admiringly at the plump face of a little French cousin, her first grandchild, whom she held on one arm. That cousin was born in France before the war.

My conjecture is that my grandmother obtained a visa to travel from Germany to France as a tourist in 1937 to see her daughter, new granddaughter, and perhaps the Paris World's Fair. She may have seen the light show at the Fair, when the Eiffel Tower was illuminated with 10,000 neon lights in three different colors. I doubt that she went into the German Pavilion, a massive stone tower 500 feet tall with enormous swastikas hanging on its sides, topped with the German

Eagle. But my grandmother *did* see her family in Paris in 1937. I have the picture.

And she may have seen the Spanish Pavilion at the Fair, with Picasso's painting *Guernica*, created as a protest against the German air bombardment of the city of Guernica during the Spanish Civil War.

I'll never know, though, why my grandmother returned to Germany, instead of remaining in Paris with my aunt, even after her visa expired. Was she just another obedient German subject? There were many, too many, obedient subjects who followed the rules, and that road ended for many of them in the gas chambers.

Didn't my grandmother realize how risky it was to return to Germany? It is difficult for me to believe that she didn't understand the danger. Did my grandmother even think about remaining in Paris?

When I viewed a YouTube video of the 1937 Paris World's Fair and saw the crowds strolling near the German Pavilion, surrounded by flags flapping under the swastika, I knew that somewhere in the crowd was my grandmother. I couldn't find her. I couldn't warn her not to go back to Germany. I was helpless.

My Jewish grandmother returned to nazi Germany with a present for my father, a tie from the 1937 Paris World's Fair; the one that hung by itself in my father's closet.

Chapter 17

Kristallnacht 2008

My dream began November 5, 2008. Just before I left home for the airport, I checked my email one last time. There was a note from Frau Krenn. She wished me a good trip and wrote that she had been able to look in the Leipzig cemetery book, which she said was old, hand-written, and difficult to read. However, there was a reference to my grandfather's grave, which said the stone was not readable. That saddened me a bit because I was hoping the tombstone would have the name of my great-grandfather, a gold nugget in the genealogical search for my family, a link to my past.

I wondered why the stone was in such bad condition. My grandfather died in 1929, and that wasn't so long ago for a slab of granite, unless the stone had been desecrated. My hope was she was looking at the wrong grave marker.

It was 3:32 p.m. on that November day, and I was seated in 20C, in a winged time machine headed for Paris, the first leg of my trip to Leipzig. In my knapsack, in the overhead compartment, were my father's phylacteries —tefillin in Yiddish. Tefillin are ritual objects worn by Jewish men during morning prayer services. For about sixty years, they had lived in a red satin bag hidden in the suitcase in my father's closet. My grandmother had made that bag, and I wanted to carry it home for him.

Initially, I hesitated to take it with me because my grandmother had embroidered a large Star of David on its front, and I didn't want to have to discuss the Jewish Star with a customs inspector or border guard in Germany. I was afraid it would identify me as a Jew. It made me think of my father's passport, branded with the red letters, identifying him as a JEW. But, I figured that if my father had carried the bag with the star through nazi Germany on Kristallnacht in 1938, I could carry it through the European Union seventy years later. It struck me, though, how important being Jewish was to my father.

I wedged my clarinet into a space in the overhead bin where I thought it would be insulated from rough air bumps and landing bounces. I wanted to give it a comfortable ride, for it had an important part to play in my dream.

At 7:30 the following morning, the plane landed in a dense fog at Charles DeGaulle Airport, Paris. I was looking out the window for signs of a city, but the first evidence of the ground was the bump when the wheels hit the runway. When we exited the plane, we were met in the jetway by a woman who said in her French-accented English, "We must go very quickly to the connecting flight to Berlin."

I had every intention of doing so. I didn't want to be late for my dream. About two hours later I was in Tegel Airport, Berlin, where I took a taxi to the Hotel Jurine in the Prenzlauer Berg section of the city.

David was waiting in the lobby, wearing a fuzzy gray ski cap, an old leather jacket, and carrying a newspaper in a white plastic bag. We hugged.

"I'm dreaming," I said.

"Are you tired?" he asked.

"No, I'm pumped."

"Are you hungry?"

"A little."

"Then let's go to the corner; there's a little café." He adjusted his fuzzy cap as we stepped through the doors of the hotel. In the café I was tempted to ask David to translate one of the letters I was carrying, but I wanted to save that for Leipzig. I was eager to be a tourist in Berlin, and to see how long I could hold out before jetlag overtook me.

David and I walked through Berlin, tracing the path of the Berlin Wall. We visited the newly inaugurated Rykestrasse synagogue, built in 1904, used as a stable by the Wehrmacht during the war and restored slowly over the years. We met a friend of David's, Inga, a native German, and we walked to the new Holocaust museum near the American Embassy. It made me think of hitler's wish to build a museum to the "Extinct Race," but I was happy to refute him in his backyard. On a drizzling night, hundreds of black marble blocks, some towering over us, glistened in the rain. The monuments stood silently in rows of narrow alleyways on pathways that rose and fell. The memorials had no names or addresses, like the anonymous victims who perished in the war. We went downstairs into the museum, where a quote from Primo Levi hung on the wall.

"If it happened, it can happen again."

I knew the Holocaust story, but I didn't know why I was attracted to these places that kept tugging on my insides.

After some time in the museum, we continued through the Berlin night. Then suddenly, David ran halfway down the street to a plaque fixed to a pole in the ground. He was looking at his map and pointing back toward the building behind us.

"This is where hitler's bunker was," he said. I turned and found myself facing a neon-lit storefront.

"What do you think hitler would say if he knew his bunker was a Chinese restaurant?" I asked.

David and I laughed. Inga looked disturbed. "I don't understand how Jews can joke about that. I would never say such a thing," she said.

As we walked and talked, Inga asked me about my father.

"He lived in Leipzig until Kristallnacht," I said. "Then he came to America. He lived in New York City, in a place called Washington Heights, where there were so many German refugees my father said they referred to the neighborhood as the "Fourth Reich.""

Inga gave me the same look as when I had made the comment about hitler's bunker. I guess some humor is best understood by those of a similar stripe.

I was getting tired. I figured I had been up for about twenty-four hours, so I said my goodbyes, got in a cab, and headed back to the hotel. In my room, I sat on the bed and immediately felt my exhaustion mix with the excited anticipation of being in Leipzig the next day. My eyelids were heavy.

I am standing across the street from my grandmother's house. The air is clear; the night comes easily with the cold. I am self-conscious about opening up my clarinet case on the sidewalk. There are just a few people on the street. I lift my clarinet and begin to play. My fingers are cold; I play slowly at first, deliberately, each note in its own space.

The sound swirls around me with the snowflakes. The sky is dark, but the street is brighter. People walk toward me. They are drawn to the music. They have no color, or rather they are not colorful. They are gray or green. The people look as if they are made of clay, but they have human mannerisms. They are covered not with dirt but with earth. Most are barefoot and wear rags. I am not scared, but curious. Despite the cold they are not shivering. It does not occur to me that maybe those people are not living.

I am now playing as loudly as I can play. A woman steps forward from the crowd. She is wrapped in a blanket. Her arm is extended, and she wants to hand me something. It is a letter in an envelope. Its edge is ragged; it had been torn open. It comes to me that these people are prisoners. They form a circle around me and begin to dance. A violin player steps from the crowd. We play a klezmer tune together.

I smell bread baking. Tables are set for a banquet. More musicians come. A veiled woman and a man in a silk top hat stand in front of a rabbi who signals us to stop playing. My grandmother comes out from her house across the street. She has tears in her eyes as she walks past me. I have come all this way to see her, but she does not see me. We are like trains on different tracks.

I don't know how many times the phone rang. It took me a moment to figure out where I was and why I had woken up fully clothed, with my shoes on. David was on the phone. He was waiting downstairs. It was breakfast time in Berlin.

Friday morning November 7, David and I boarded the train to Leipzig. David read me a newspaper article about anti-Semitism in Germany as the train ran through some uneventful countryside. In the article, a German rabbi said how central the synagogue was to the practice of Judaism. The nazis also knew that on Kristallnacht, I thought. We stopped once or twice before slowing to a stop at the Leipzig Hauptbahnhof (Hbf), the main train station.

When I emerged onto the platform and stood beside the sign, Leipzig Hbf, I dropped my belongings in a pile and began to cry. This was the last place both my father and grandmother stood in Leipzig. I felt the spirits of my family and those of the thousands of others for whom this was the beginning of life's end.

We bought a street map in the train station, then left our bags at the hotel. In the lobby, I spied a welcome sign for a Dr. Mengel, and the woman who checked us in had "Borman" on her nametag. Maybe I was a little touchy about being greeted with the names of former nazis. David and I located 10 Lohrstrasse on the map, the office of Frau Krenn, and five minutes later I rang her doorbell.

"Ah, yes, Herr Bein," said the voice on the intercom.

A beautiful part about being in Germany was that the Germans always pronounced my last name correctly. In the United States, I'd given up correcting the assortment of tortured mispronunciations.

For some time, I had wondered what Frau Krenn looked like, and there she was at the top of the stairs, a woman my age, in jeans, wearing a broad smile.

"Which one of you is Mr. Bein?" she said.

I introduced myself and David. We shook hands.

"Come in, come in, my English is not so good what I wrote you."

"It was perfect," I said.

"Nothing is perfect," she said, as she led us swiftly through the open door.

"This is my office." Her arm swept an arc across her desk and some tables covered with papers. There were some wooden file cabinets, a couple of pictures on the wall, and three windows, lit by a gray sky.

"I have prepared something for you. Come sit," said Frau Krenn. "But first I have a request. *Ich möchte Sie bitten, das Gästebuch zu unterzeichnen.*"

"She wants you to sign the guestbook," David explained.

Frau Krenn went to a cabinet and took the last thin volume from a row of books labeled 1933, 1934, 1935. She opened it in front of me. I saw the names of other visitors, relatives of the 1938 Leipzig Jewish Community, now located in Europe, Israel, the United States, and South America. I added my name to the history: Peter Bein, son of Max Bein, grandson of Malka and Hirsch Bein of 18 Uferstrasse.

"One good thing about the Holocaust; it dispersed us all over the world. We are not so much all in the same place," Frau Krenn said. I could identify with her feeling of collective safety. "They can't find us all so easily if we are spread out."

She paused. "I have something for you." She placed an envelope on the table. "From 1935."

Inside were four green cards, forms filled out neatly in fountain pen. My eyes must have popped out of my head. The original membership cards from the synagogue with the names of my father Max, my grandmother Malka, my great-uncle Selig, and my aunt Sidonia lay before me. To anyone else they were just paper cards, but Frau Krenn knew she had just offered me the Hope Diamond. I gathered up the cards and held them with both hands over my heart. Seventy years blew by. My family had just left the office. There was only one door, one way in and one way out, but somehow I missed them.

I handed the cards to David. "My family's membership from 1935." *His* eyes looked like they were going to pop out of *his* head.

"What a coincidence," he said. I didn't tell him I didn't believe in coincidences.

I took my grandmother's card, the one with "Malka" written in a very ornate hand.

"Is this her handwriting?" I asked Frau Krenn.

She shook her head. She could tell I was disappointed.

I couldn't believe what had just happened. A few months ago, in Atlanta, I had stepped into the time machine when I sent an email inquiring about Leipzig. Someone in Berlin picked up the message and told me to contact Frau Krenn. Thirty minutes ago I had walked into her office. It just happened to be in the synagogue that my family attended seventy years ago, the only one that survived on Kristallnacht, and I was presented with their membership cards, circa 1935.

"Do you know the names Degen and Frauwirt from Leipzig?" I asked her. "They were my cousins." She pointed to a stack of wooden file drawers that looked like the card catalog in an old library.

"You can look yourself. They are in alphabetical order," she said in a way that sounded like *Don't mess them up.*

"I'll keep them in order," I assured her.

I found the cards of a half-dozen relatives, five of them killed by the nazis. I was panting as if I had run five miles.

"Today I am very busy, but you can come back Monday, and you can look more," Frau Krenn said. She looked me up and down.

"I thought you'd be a seventy-year-old man. Your father was born in 1911."

"He had me late in life. I'm fifty-four."

But I needed the laugh with Frau Krenn.

"Let me show you what I found in the cemetery for your grandfather," she said.

She pointed to a diagram.

"It will be very difficult to find, but a member of the community will go with you. It is either row four or row twenty-six, depending which end of the cemetery you enter. It will be near these," and she gave me a list of names.

"Mr. Finemann will be in the synagogue this evening. He will help you find your grandfather's grave. Are you religious?"

"A little," I said. I had always found that question difficult to answer.

"The service here is not so religious. The community is all Russian Jews. There are no German Jews here anymore."

"I read about a Mr. Isaacson from Leipzig on the internet," I said. "Wasn't he a young boy on Kristallnacht?"

Frau Krenn nodded. "Yes, and later he was the leader of this community. He would speak every November 9, but he doesn't anymore. He's tired of talking about it."

"So, they're all Russians?" I said, referring to the new community.

"The community is different from the way it was. My boss used to come into my office, an old German, and he was strong. If a drawer was open or a closet was open, he would yell. Now things are different." She made two fists and mimed banging on the table.

She opened the folder from which she had taken my family's membership cards and the cemetery map.

"Here; there is one more thing. Do you know it?"

She handed me another piece of paper, a typed letter. At first glance it looked familiar, but any typewriter could have banged out a page of Times New Roman font with a worn ribbon, I thought. But when I looked closer, I had that feeling that one sometimes gets when the brain doesn't want to believe what the eyes are seeing. The letter was written by my father to the synagogue in 1964. It ended with his unmistakable signature. Frau Krenn saw the question in my face.

"Your father needed proof that he had been a member of this community and was asking the synagogue for a reference."

I slapped the tabletop so hard with my palm, it stung my hand. David and Frau Krenn jumped.

"He knew about this place," I said, poking a finger into the letter. "He knew this synagogue was here. Why didn't he tell me?"

"Did you ever ask him?" Frau Krenn said.

"No. He didn't like to talk about it."

She waved her hand at the cabinet containing the visitors' logs.

"I have heard *that* before," she said.

♦

It was time to go.

"Will you come to the ceremony on Sunday?" Frau Krenn asked, referring to the city's commemoration of Kristallnacht.

"I'll be there."

She walked us to the door.

"Have you seen where your father lived?"

"Not yet. It's getting dark soon," I said. "I'll go tomorrow after synagogue."

"It's very close. Just two streets." She pointed. "Go there and then there."

That evening I attended Friday night services at the Broyder Synagogue, just around the corner from Frau Krenn's office. It was, as my research said, built into the lower level of an apartment house, a detail that had saved it from the arsonist's torch on Kristallnacht. Its interior was decorated in the Moorish style, the ornate molding accented in blue and gold, and the circular stained-glass windows protected on the street side by iron filigree. There was seating downstairs for about one hundred men. White pillars supported a smaller women's section in the upstairs balcony. But I got goosebumps when I thought about my father being here, and I stared up into the balcony, searching for my grandmother.

I thought she might be wearing that black hat, sitting at a rakish angle, as I remember from her picture that lived in the suitcase. Resting in her lap is a pair of thin leather gloves. But why is she sitting alone, looking so solemn, her lips taut? She has a distant gaze, as though she is looking for something far off.

And as Frau Krenn said, the congregants were all Russian. We couldn't talk to each other, but somehow I met Mr. Finemann. A thin man, younger than I, approached me after the service. He must have been on the lookout for a stranger.

"My name Grisha," he said, pointing to himself.

He spoke a few words of English, and we both spoke a few words of Hebrew. With those few words and some sign language, we arranged to meet on Sunday. He would take me to the cemetery to find my grandfather's grave. I couldn't help but feel like I was dreaming.

After synagogue services, David and I met at the hotel and then had dinner at the Caffe Baum, a restaurant that first served coffee at that location in Leipzig in 1694. I ordered sauerbraten, red cabbage, and potato dumplings, and the taste transported me back to my mother's table forty years earlier, when she often served my father this same dinner. Gazing around the restaurant, I wondered where my father had sat, if indeed he weren't here right now. I wished he were.

"Don't you get bored praying, saying the same words over and over again in synagogue?" asked David, who is Jewish but probably had not seen the inside of a synagogue in a while.

"David, you heathen. I sat in a room with thirty Russian men. We spoke different languages. But we said the same words in our prayers, we sang the same songs. Our fathers sang those songs. We connected. We connected to each other and to something larger."

The next morning, I returned to the Broyder Synagogue for the Sabbath service. Yesterday's open door was a locked iron gate, which fit my expectation of what I thought security in a German synagogue might be. I knocked on the window, and a congregant came outside and let me in. Soon after being seated, I was called for an honor at the Torah, where I chanted the blessing before the rabbi read the week's portion from the scroll of the law. I read the blessings loudly and carefully. My father was listening. I was on his home turf. But the weekly portion contained the story of how G-d told Abraham to go out of the land and the house of his father. I didn't know how to take that, being that I was doing the exact opposite, and I had come so far.

After the service I met a young Russian man in the synagogue who spoke a little English. I told him that my family belonged here seventy years ago. He listened. I told him how happy I was to have seen their membership cards, how much they meant to me.

"I see absolutely no reason for them to have kept those cards for so long. How Yekkish [German] of them," he said.

He used the word Yekka, for German, a derogatory term that Jews from Eastern Europe, Poland, and Russia used to describe German Jews. He chose a pointed word, especially on the seventieth anniversary of Kristallnacht, in Leipzig, Germany, where not so long ago, Yekka or not, all Jews were hunted. But I didn't take offense. It was the Sabbath, and I was in my father's synagogue.

As we were leaving the service, the Russian congregants motioned for me to follow them. Grisha, who was locking up, said to me, "Go wis them. I meet you."

I followed the congregation, men and women, down the street and around the corner into a meeting hall where I watched them prepare Sabbath lunch. I couldn't talk with anyone and waited, leaning on a back wall, hands in my pockets, occasionally checking the time, while they hurried in and out of the kitchen with plates of fish, salads, eggs, cheese, and some things I couldn't identify. They motioned for me to sit. Men sat on one side, women on the other. The leader of the community opened a bottle of something Scotch-like, said the blessing, and passed the bottle for a "L'Chaim" toast. We ate, and drank, and sang Sabbath songs.

It didn't matter that I couldn't talk with anyone. I was with family.

After lunch I walked in the direction Frau Krenn had pointed me, toward Uferstrasse, my family's street. Ufer means riverbank, and when I saw the narrow river, I knew I had to be in the right vicinity because of a story that gushed into my mind. My father grew up during the period of hyperinflation after World War I, when the value of German money decreased hourly.

"As young boys," he had told me, "we used to ask the shopkeepers for their small bills. The bills were worthless. We played with the paper money, and when we were finished playing, we'd throw the money in the river."

I was standing by that river, only separated by about eighty years. The river was so narrow.

I kept walking and saw Uferstrasse on the street sign. I knew the house had to be near, and I began to run, looking for number eighteen. But the buildings looked too modern. I kept going. Then across the road I saw it on a glass pane in a large wooden door. "18."

There stood a three-story building, with wrought iron balconies hung under the windows on the upper floors. A decorative stone just below the roofline of the house adorned with "1895" said, "This is the place."

Oblivious to the traffic, I dashed across the street. I touched the door and rubbed the "18" with my fingertips. It was a reflex, as though seeing was not enough and just being in that place was not enough. I needed a physical connection to my father's house. I wanted to know what it knew, what it had seen, half-thinking I could feel the stories within, through my fingertips. For one more moment, I kept my hand on the glass pane. Had the street been empty, I might have lingered at my father's door and connected with his house. In the literal sense, it was a "touching moment" that gave me more of an appreciation for the expression, "staying in touch."

Seeing my father's house for the first time and touching the spot where my grandmother had lived connected me to something primitive. Somehow this place was imprinted on me. No one had asked me to come. No one had expected me to come, quite the opposite. But now, being in that spot was the right thing. I could feel it down to the marrow in my bones.

I had no choice. I was pulled here. And while we were forced to flee from here in a flood of refugees seventy years ago, for a moment I knew how fish or turtles could travel thousands of miles to find their way home, perhaps by recognizing a familiar magnetic tug.

I stood at my father's door and wondered what else to do. Was I a tourist? Why would posing for pictures feel so odd? What gesture could be offered to this place? My clarinet would have been perfect, but I couldn't get into my grandmother's house where I had heard myself play a klezmer song for her. I wanted the music to cover the walls and ceilings and rise up out of the chimney into the skies. Maybe the vibrations would stir something in an old closet or in my father's favorite hiding place. Perhaps in the basement, near the potato bin, there was an old trunk with a story to tell.

I stood under my grandmother's window and could have thrown pebbles against the glass to make her come and look down into the street, see me wave and open the door. I could look through the outer door and see into the courtyard. If someone came out, I might be able to go inside and see my family's apartment on the third floor.

I waited. The outer door never opened. I walked up and down the street and came back and stood at the door again. I don't know how long I leaned on the wall and watched the cars go by. I kicked myself for not having prepared better for this moment, for not having contacted the building's residents before I arrived. But I remembered that my internet research showed a software company at this address, not two neat rows of name-labels, Krause, Neumann, Braun, Langer, and Winkler, beside black buttons near the intercom.

After a while I realized I was going to have to surrender being able to play a klezmer song for my grandmother inside her apartment. It was a defeat, but I didn't feel as though I had come to her door for nothing. My grandmother knew I was there to see her. Don't grandmothers know things like that?

My father's school was a ten-minute walk from his house on Uferstrasse. I passed a park and a large meadow. The park was beside the zoo, about which my father had spoken so often. His favorites were the monkeys. The field I stood beside must have been where my father played soccer as a boy and chased after the ball made of wound-up rags. He told me they were all too poor to afford a proper soccer ball. The game was often interrupted to retie the rags.

And one day my father had dilly-dallied on that field. He told me his mother had given him a bag filled with paper money, more than enough to buy a loaf of bread at the bakery, even during that period of inflation. On the way to the bakery he stopped to play soccer with his friends. By the time he got to the store, the price of the bread had doubled, and he didn't have enough money. He had to return home empty-handed. He said his mother was never so angry at him as she was that day.

I sat on the steps of the Carlebach Haus, the home of the Leipzig School for the Blind. Seventy years earlier my father had been a student here, when it was the Carlebach School, founded by Rabbi Ephriam Carlebach. I thought of my adolescent father and his friends behaving poorly out here on the steps, between classes. There he was with Alfred from across the courtyard. I could feel their presence.

A hand on my back at that moment made me jump. For a moment the experience was too real. But it wasn't my father or Alfred. I was blocking the path of a student leaving school and had to catch him when he stumbled.

As I walked through what once was my father's world, his little community, I recognized street names I had last seen on the envelopes that lived in his hidden suitcase. A cousin lived on Humboldtstrasse, a five-minute walk from my family's apartment. My father worked on Richard Wagner Strasse, ten minutes away. His synagogue was a little further than around the corner; his school, ten minutes away.

That world was small, and I was in it. A relaxed, comfortable feeling came over me. For some reason, I felt safer. Finally, I knew where my father had grown up. I had punctured what, to me, was a long-lived secret. In reality, my father didn't have anything to hide, but this place was just too painful for him to remember.

◆

That evening, seven euro got David and me seats in the corner of the four-hundred-year-old St. Thomaskirche for the Mozart *Requiem*. I sat thirty feet from Bach, his final resting place. The piece began; the music was smooth and sweet. There was some tension, a wash of sound, some back and forth between the orchestra and choir. I heard a clarinet's voice call to me through the powerful timpani and brass across the cavernous cathedral, whose ceiling was buttressed in the Gothic style, with red wooden ribs. We were in the rib cage of a huge beast. Then came four-part harmony, and then the choir and orchestra suddenly stopped. The sweet sounds kept on, floated for a moment on the air before they disappeared, unsupported. The silence between movements was disturbed by people in the audience who had waited to clear their throats and rearrange themselves in their chairs.

A trombone labored behind a bass solo, the choir cried out. The music laughed at me, and something inside me boiled. How could such a horrible thing have happened in a place where people enjoyed such a beautiful composition? My heart pounded, or was that the timpani?

A crucifix hung on the wall above, and Christ looked down on me. The choir ended in a minor key. I felt exhausted. Two days before in Berlin, I had thought of forgiveness. A few hours ago, on my father's street, I felt some comfort. Now I was angry. How did this church escape being bombed flat in the war, as other parts of the city were? Would it have been considered too barbaric for the Allies to bomb a church? On the night before Kristallnacht, did the nazis listen to Mozart?

The next morning David and I met Grisha outside the synagogue. He motioned for us to follow him to the trolley. He was going to take us to the Jewish cemetery. We were joined by a group of men on the trolley stop, Russian congregants of the synagogue. We played charades to find out that one trolley ticket works for two people on a Sunday, and we didn't need to buy any extra tickets.

After a twenty-minute ride, we left the trolley, and

I saw the cemetery across the street. As I approached the black iron gate, I felt as though the air had gotten thick and syrupy, as if there an invisible heaviness was holding me back. But I had traveled so far to get here, I just pushed my way through.

I had the directions Frau Krenn provided, but they didn't mean anything to me. I started walking up and down the aisles, looking for my grandfather's grave. A man in a black suit and black shirt materialized out of nowhere and took the map from my hand.

He said, "I'll find it," and then he walked away.

He returned in five minutes and motioned for me to follow. We walked down a number of aisles and then he pointed and said, "Hirsch Bein."

The stone was beautifully polished, and I thought: How could this be the one? It was very different from what Frau Krenn's description had led me to believe. I came around to the front and read my grandfather's name. The man in the black suit disappeared as quickly as he had come. The inscription on the stone was partly in German and partly in Hebrew. David translated the German: "Here lies my dear and faithful husband and dependable father." My grandfather died on the operating table in 1929, when my father was eighteen.

The story goes, my father did not get on well with his father, which is probably why I knew next-to-nothing about Hirsch. And while my DNA is partly his, I knew from the only, lonely picture I had of my grandfather, I didn't resemble him. So, as I stood teary-eyed in front of his grave, I needed more of a connection to this dead stranger. I remembered when I had been squeaking and squawking, learning to play the clarinet, my father told me that his father taught himself the violin, which he'd play on Friday nights, before going to synagogue. I immediately cherished our musical connection.

I picked out my great-grandfather's name from the Hebrew inscription on the gravestone. "Israel Yudel," I repeated. "Israel Yudel." Perhaps my words that hung in the air gave his spirit a place to rest. Who knew the last time his name was spoken? Maybe it had not been heard since my grandfather's funeral in 1929, maybe not since his own funeral.

The Russian congregants and I said Kaddish, the prayer for the dead, and the men left me to be alone with my grandfather. I placed some pebbles on his tombstone, the custom when visiting a Jewish cemetery. I dried my eyes. Later, I found out that the man who had helped me find my grandfather's grave was Mr. Isaacson, the fellow I had read about on the internet, the young boy from Leipzig, Kristallnacht 1938.

On November 9, 2008, David and I stood on a street corner in Leipzig and watched as a young woman approached from across the cobblestone street. She held out a microphone and said something to us in German.

"The local radio station is taking a survey. Do you know what happened here seventy years ago?" David translated through a chuckle. I could make out his answer, as he pointed to me and told the interviewer, "His Jewish father lived in Leipzig until Kristallnacht."

I thought: "How could she ask me such a thing?" My answer could fill the pages of a book.

Her German sounded harsh. It was the familiar language my father had spoken, and at the same time it was the cruel language of the nazis. As I stood on the sidewalk, it reminded me that in my father's day, in this place, Jewish people were forbidden to use the sidewalks.

Later in the afternoon, I attended a Kristallnacht commemoration. The uberburgermeister addressed a crowd gathered for the ceremony at the Stadtburo. He was blond, with angular features, tall and standing arrow-straight. A church bell rang, and the mayor spoke. David translated. The mayor said it wasn't just the fault of the nazis, it was the regular citizens who took part as well. He lit a candle emblazoned with a Star of David. He said we must remember even seventy years from now. He spoke at length to the 150 who were present in this city of more than 500,000 people.

Following the mayor's address, there was a ceremony around the corner from my family's house on the Parthe River, at a monument to the victims of the Holocaust. As we approached the monument, a blaring voice from a loudspeaker came out of the sky: "*Wo ist dein bruder?*" "Where is your brother?" It was the inscription on the memorial stone. The Biblical reference from the Cain and Abel story sounded odd. How could G-d have spoken German?

Only about a hundred people were present at the wreath-laying near the Parthe. We heard a Holocaust witness tell the story of a little boy asking his grandfather on that night why the firemen weren't putting out the fire in the synagogue, but just standing beside the fire truck.

hitler had said that he wanted to extinguish the Jews and make a museum in their memory. I felt like I was part of an exhibit in that museum, as I had at the Holocaust memorial in Berlin. hitler had made his point.

At 9 p.m. on Kristallnacht, November 9, 2008, I sat in the balcony of my father's synagogue listening to the Leipziger Synagogal Choir present a Gedenkkonzert, a memorial concert. They performed Yiddische Gesange and Synagogenmusik, and there was not an empty seat. The house lights were out, and the eternal flame in the sanctuary illuminated the synagogue with an orange, fire like brilliance, but on this Kristallnacht, the flame did not consume.

The concert lasted about an hour, but the constant applause didn't let the choir end its performance without a number of encores. I was smiling so much my face hurt.

We knew what had happened here seventy years ago.

Chapter 18

Stumbling Stones

The afternoon following the commemoration, we discussed the Kristallnacht ceremonies and the mayor's speech in Frau Krenn's office.

"I was touched by how deeply many Christians I've met felt for the plight of the Jews in the Holocaust. Their feelings were so genuine," I said.

She crossed her arms.

"Sometimes I think so too, but you know, now it is very fashionable to know Jews in Leipzig. We are like the monkeys in the zoo."

Her words hung in the air.

Frau Krenn broke the silence. "You may be interested in this." She picked through a pile of papers on her desk, then handed me a magazine article. We held it between us as she translated the story.

"There is a German sculptor, Gunter Demnig, who lives in Cologne. His art is called Stolperstein, or stumbling stones. He creates the stones to give a name to those murdered by the nazis. A Stolperstein is a four-inch cube of concrete topped with a brass plate that carries a simple inscription beginning with "Hier wohnte...," Here lived.... He puts them into the sidewalk outside the homes of Holocaust victims. Sometimes there is a little ceremony. Look on the streets near here. You may see one. Would you be interested in doing something like that for your grandmother?"

I did want my grandmother's name to finally have a home; I just had to get used to the idea of people walking on it. I nodded slowly.

"I can help you arrange it through Achim Beier, the Archivist of the City. He is in charge of the project."

Frau Krenn called him on the phone, and they spoke for a few minutes. During their conversation, I warmed up to the idea of my grandmother's name set in a sidewalk when I thought about the Walk of Fame, underfoot on Hollywood Boulevard.

"Done," she said. "You can go see him. His office is not far. I'll show you. He will ask for some information and tell you when the ceremony will take place."

"Thank you. I'd like that very much."

"What do you think about your trip to Germany?" she asked.

"I was hesitant to come here, you can understand, but from what I have seen here and in Berlin I can say that the government and some of the citizens are making amends for the past. They are feeling their guilt."

She shuffled through some papers on her desk as she listened.

"But one thing that is uncomfortable in an odd way is the language, the German language," I said.

"How so?"

"When I hear German spoken in Leipzig, with the Saxon accent, the way you speak, it is a very familiar, comfortable sound. It is the language that my father spoke. But when I hear the same language on the loudspeaker in the train station, for example, or from the mayor's mouth, it sounds like a cruel language, guttural, like the barking of a dog, the language of hitler."

Frau Krenn had a glint in her eye.

"I know just what you mean," she said. "You must separate the language from the crime."

♦

After leaving Frau Krenn's office I went to see Achim Beier. At 11 Katherinstrasse, I climbed the wooden spiral staircase and knocked on the door under the sign "Archiv Burgerbewgung." There was no answer, but when I turned the knob and pushed on the door it opened to a *ding-dong*. It smelled like a museum. After a moment a bearded man in his forties wearing jeans and a sweatshirt emerged from around a corner.

"You must be Herr Bein," he said.

"And you are Herr Beier," I answered.

We shook hands.

"Come in," he said.

I followed him through the small community museum

with wooden floors and stuffed bookshelves to his office in a back room. While we chatted, he told me that he was a student of history. His area of interest was the reign of the dictators who ruled Germany in the twentieth century. He told me that he leads the Stolperstein project in Leipzig.

"Frau Krenn tells me you may be interested in a Stolperstein for your grandmother."

"I didn't know about them before I came, but I would like to give my grandmother back her name, in a public way.

"I can help you arrange that," he said. "There is a Stolperstein artist in Germany who travels to three hundred German cities to plant the stones. There are already about twenty thousand of them, mostly in German sidewalks. He comes to Leipzig twice a year."

Pages flipped in the calendar in my head.

"The project is usually taken on by a schoolchild who does the research on the Holocaust victim and receives the benefit of the learning. Sometimes, as in your case, the family does the research." He waved a handwritten sheet of information about my grandmother that he had probably written during the phone call with Frau Krenn.

"Please give me your email address. I may have more questions about your grandmother. Do you have any other information about your family?"

I had brought with me some pictures and copies of letters with Leipzig addresses. I also had one original letter written by my grandmother and a letter of reference written by my father's employer in 1937. I wasn't so much interested in the reference as in the address of the firm printed on the ornate letterhead. In the 1930s, my father had worked in a Leipzig leather tannery, Simon Kahn.

As I set the artifacts on his desk, Achim's eyes got wide. One might have thought by his expression that he was looking at a table full of ten-carat diamonds. He rubbed his hands together and asked me if he could have a few minutes with the documents. While he poured over my letters, I studied the pictures on the walls of his office and at an old map of the city. After a while he looked up and said, "Okay." He put his hands together as if he were going to give me a report on what he had read.

He picked up my father's passport and showed me where it had been stamped NO RETURN upon his leaving Germany on November 10, 1938. That was a good thing, I thought. He also took the letter from my father's employer.

"This is important. May I have a copy?"

"Certainly."

"Was this business owned by a Jewish person?"

"Yes, I believe so."

"This line is important," he said, pointing to the letter. "It says that your father worked there for ten years and then left the company because it was sold."

I didn't get it. He must have seen my puzzled look.

"We know that in 1937 Jews were not allowed to own businesses, so the owner was forced to sell," Achim said. "He could not write in the letter that the nazis had forced him to sell, but we know that now to be true.

If Simon Kahn's grandson comes to Leipzig tomorrow and needs proof of the existence of his family's business, can I give him this letter?"

"Absolutely. Please do. And if he comes, I'd like to meet him. Give him my email address as well. We'd have a lot to talk about."

Achim brought the letter to the copy machine. I showed him the memory stick that contained my digitized archive. He smiled and led me to his computer.

I sat down to copy the artifacts for him, but was stymied by the German-language toolbar. He laughed and came to the rescue. While we worked together, transferring the information, he saw a picture of my father's fiancée, Lola, circa 1937.

"Who is that?" he asked.

"She was almost my mother."

A Man and His Child

My child wants to visit his grandma.
He holds her picture tight.
He must adore the woman he sees
But it's not so black and white.

He heard that she had disappeared
And thought it a trick, like magic,
But the word I know was verschwunden
And the situation tragic.

His curiosity makes demands
The boy must go this instant
He doesn't understand it's quite a trip
The destination distant.

Seventy years after Kristallnacht
He is propelled in a trance
To stand beneath her window there
And play a klezmer dance.

A man and his child boarded a plane
They disembarked in the land of the Hun,
And what you suspected you may find true
The man and his child were one.

Chapter 19

Trains

I wander and wonder in the great hall of the Leipzig train station, the Hauptbahnhof. In 1938 it was the largest in Europe. I'm looking for a connection–not a train, but a familiar spirit, a flicker of the past. My grandmother stood here, somewhere on this marble floor, before she was deported to Poland seventy years ago. If I listen, we can almost touch. She was just here, before they packed her into a cattle car with other Polish Jews, never to return. My father also stood somewhere near this bench, seventy years ago, before he escaped to America.

I can only imagine the scene on Kristallnacht. My father meets his fiancée on his last day in Leipzig at their rendezvous spot in the station, under the clock.

Its giant, glowing face sees all in this great hall. But instead of business travelers or vacationers, the clock, my father, and Lola see long lines of anxious families waiting to purchase their tickets to travel out of Germany, to safety. The usual order and calm of the main hall is broken by the shouts of mothers trying to keep scrambling children close, fathers calling their families to the next line.

Loose belongings are piled on valises. Bits and pieces spill over onto the smooth, polished floor in the grand hall of the station: a doll, a fur hat, a pair of boots. Some have packed so quickly that little bits of clothing stick out from under the lids of their suitcases, whose sides bulge like sausages. Others come to the station in such a hurry they carry no belongings, other than the clothes on their back. Escape means taking with them only that which they can carry. For some, it means putting a lifetime into a suitcase.

For those fortunate enough to a get a ticket on a train out of Germany on Kristallnacht, every moment of the ride is tuned to the clickity-clack of iron wheels across the tracks. Optimism springs as the train speeds forward to the border, but a deceleration or a sudden stop quickens the heartbeat, dries the mouth, and causes sweat to bead on the brow, even on a cold November day in Germany.

Some weeks before Kristallnacht, my father had actually been on such a train, bound for Switzerland. It left from this station. He said all the travelers were trying to escape. Spirits rose as they approached the Swiss border and safety. But just before the border, the train came to a stop. Passengers pressed their faces to the windows to see what was happening. There was no train station. German soldiers boarded the cars, hauled off some passengers, and reversed the train, back to Leipzig. My father said, "Not one word was spoken during the trip back. A trainload of our Jewish people with death sentences. Most of them didn't survive the war."

How they hung their heads when their train came back into the Hauptbahnhof. Was it track 11 over there, or 16, where they trudged?

♦

While wandering in the station, another story rushed at me. Sometime around 1964, my brother and I heard that we were going to get some money. First, I overheard the news in a telephone conversation between my mother, in our Brooklyn kitchen, and my father in Manhattan. The following day I heard my father on the phone to his sister in Paris. That was rare, and it made me think something was up. International calling was expensive in the early sixties, not always person-to-person, but through an international operator, making it tricky to complete a call.

I remember during that particular conversation my father was happy, excited, talking loudly, then very quietly, listening, his lips drawn in, his hand covering the bottom of his face. But I couldn't understand the German.

A few days later, when my mother called my brother and me to the dinner table, I noticed a different inflection in her voice. She was serious. Something was going on.

"You boys are going to get some money," she said. "Your Aunt Jeanette in Paris sent a letter."

"Money? How much?" I asked.

My mother looked across the table at my father, wanting him to answer. He was staring down at his soup bowl as though it had a deep hole in the bottom and he could look through it to some far-off place. It was not out of the ordinary for my father to be physically present, but silent and really somewhere else.

My mother called to him. "Max...Max. A penny for your thoughts."

He didn't look up. She went over to him and put a hand on his shoulder. She called him by his Yiddish name.

"Nu, Meyer Lazer?"

Then my father looked up and came back into our kitchen in Brooklyn, 1964. He didn't understand or hadn't heard my mother call him. He looked up at her, puzzled, like a little boy. I didn't know where he had gone then, but now I know. He was thinking about his mother.

"Pop, how much money are we getting from Aunt Jeanette?"

"How do you know you're getting money from my sister?"

"Ma just told us. It's in the letter." I pointed to the gray airmail envelope, stamped Par Avion, under his elbow.

"How much Pop? How much is it?"

My mother said, "We don't know exactly. It's really not so much money. It won't make you a Rockefeller. You won't be able to retire."

"Why is Aunt Jeanette giving us the money?" I asked.

"She doesn't want it," my mother said. Those words seemed to have leaked out of her mouth. She looked to my father. Her face looked strained.

My father muttered something under his breath in Yiddish. He said moykhl, which means, no, thanks.

The air in the kitchen had grown uncomfortably close. The electric light became more intense.

"Why does she want to give it to the boys? Why does she want them involved?" my father asked my mother.

The word "involved" made it sound as if I was getting tangled into a mysterious plot.

"Why doesn't she give the money to her nieces?" he said.

I felt my new fortune slipping away even before I had it in my possession.

"They don't want the money," my mother said.

"Then why us?" I asked.

"Maybe your Aunt Jeanette wants to keep the money in the family," my mother said.

"Moykhl," my father said again, this time a little louder.

My mother reached over and put her hand on mine.

"I'll make a long story short." She took a deep breath. "A long time ago Pop's mother had a little store, in Germany. She lost it during the war."

"What type of store?" I asked.

My mother looked at my father again. He wasn't home.

"It was a little store. I think it was something like... a small bakery."

"How did she lose it?"

"Jewish people weren't allowed to own businesses. The nazis took it from her. Now the German government is trying to repay the families of those people whose property was taken."

By this point, my father had both elbows on the table, his head in his hands.

"Your Aunt Jeanette didn't want her share of the money. She's giving it to you and your brother. It's about $600. You can put it in your little savings account."

"Can I spend it?"

"Well, Pop doesn't want you to spend it, but I think that you can spend the interest that the money earns in the bank every year. The interest is put on your account at the end of the year, so let's say that you can buy yourself a Chanukah present."

"How much money can I use?"

My math teacher mother took up a pencil and her canary-yellow legal pad, which always seemed to be within her reach, and did a little figuring. But before she could answer, my father, the forerunner of the electronic calculator, said, "Twenty-eight dollars."

I didn't know about my connection to trains back then. Now I find it ironic that with the reparations money from Germany that my aunts or my father wouldn't take, I bought a Lionel electric train set with the 027-gauge track. Trains carried my father to safety and my grandmother to exile.

In 1964 I didn't know about blood money or dirty money, but now I understand why my father and my aunts didn't want money from the German government. It was money that was supposed to make things even in the cosmic balance. But how could it?

I cried when I stood in the Leipzig Hauptbahnhof on Kristallnacht, November 9, seventy years after my father's escape. I was flooded by these stories. They forced their way into my brain in a flash. The rattle of the trains and the excitement of the station was in my blood, as if I had inherited the memory.

I got a chill in my scalp, running down my spine and across the back of my arms, when I stood under the giant white clock with the black hands high up on the wall in the Hauptbahnhof, November 11. I thought of Lola. Was I supposed to meet her here? Was I supposed to tell her something? I couldn't remember. Did my father leave something here for me that I needed to collect?

I left Leipzig on Tuesday, November 11. As my train raced its shadow across the fields toward Berlin, wind turbines appeared in the distance, looking like a flock of prehistoric birds. I listened to adorable blond children speaking German.

Seventy years ago, when my father's train chugged away from Leipzig towards freedom, his stomach must have knotted every time the engine slowed. On that day he left something behind, more than his house, more than his possessions. He left a piece of his soul with his fiancée.

When she stood on the platform outside the window of his train and waved goodbye to my father, not knowing if they would see each other again, she tried not to cry. I thought of the postcard from the International Red Cross I had found in my father's old suitcase, the one with her name and the word "Auschwitz." But at least they had been able to say goodbye. He didn't even have that chance for a last word or last hug with his mother.

I had stood in the spot where my father and my grandmother had stood so many years earlier. That was my goal. I felt as if I had won the marathon, and I could hear my history cheering. I was on a journey that had bolted from my father's suitcase. And although returning to Uferstrasse 18 seventy years later wasn't quite revenge, it was sweet, so sweet.

Seventy years later on Armistice Day, I tried to make peace with this German place.

Chapter 20

A Song for Malka

My grandmother never had a funeral. She was murdered in a concentration camp, departing from this world without leaving a footprint. Her name was not chiseled in stone, preserved on some marker. And although my father loved his mother, he couldn't talk about her. It was too painful. As if she were a criminal, my grandmother's name was never spoken in our home. I discovered her name was Malka only by reading the letters in the suitcase. I was fifty years old before I had a discussion with any family member about my grandmother, Malka Bein. Her name had not appeared in public in at least seventy years.

I connected with Gunter Demnig's respect for forgotten names. He struck the names into brass-covered stone cubes he embedded into the cobblestones in front of the victims' residences. Demnig hoped the stone might engage passers-by to think about what had happened to those people. And through the stone, the nameless victims of the nazis - the Jews, the Communists, the homosexuals, the disabled, and the Gypsies who vanished during the war—would be remembered as humans once again, through a simple inscription beginning with, "Hier wohnte..."

Back in the United States, in the spring of 2009, I received an email from Achim Beier, the Archivist of the City of Leipzig. The service to dedicate a Stolperstein for my grandmother would take place on Friday, August 21, at twelve noon, in front of her 1938 apartment.

Uferstr. 18

12.00 Uhr Malka Bein ist mit vielen anderen Juden polnischer Herkunft am 28.10.1938 nach Polen abgeschoben worden. Ihre Kinder konnten sich durch die Auswanderung retten. 1942 bricht jeglicher Kontakt ab. Frau Bein wurde in Belzyce ermordet.

At 12 o'clock at Uferstrasse 18 - Malka Bein was deported to Poland with many other Jews of Polish origin on October 28, 1938. Her children saved themselves by emigrating. In 1942 all contact with her breaks off. Frau Bein was murdered in Belzyce.

The full schedule for August 21 showed other

Stolpersteine to be set in place that day. They would commemorate: a family of six, a communist, a teacher and his kin, a mother and her son. But the two words that would make me travel 6,000 miles, when it would have been far easier for me just to stay at home, were "Malka Bein." Now her name was going to be out in the sunlight, not just on the back of envelopes hidden in the dark in a suitcase. And, on behalf of the city, I was warmly invited to attend the ceremony.

I was charmed by the last line of the invitation. A musician was going to play for the event. I took *that* to be an invitation for *my* klezmer clarinet also. Music was appropriate. As I hadn't been able to get inside my grandmother's apartment to play for her on Kristallnacht, and I just hadn't felt I could take my clarinet and stand out on the street and wail, I would play for her this time.

But what would I play for my grandmother on August 21 on the clarinet that my father had bought me more than forty years earlier in that Brooklyn pawn shop? It didn't make any sense to think that he knew would one day be playing it in front of his house.

My grandmother didn't speak a word of English, and I not a word of German, but maybe the clarinet would become my voice for a moment and the music would float upward and find its way to that place where other things cannot go.

Notes from my clarinet played in my head: some sharp, some loud, some sweet. A proclamation. I thought of the blasts of the shofar, the ram's horn, on the Day of Atonement, a Biblical battle cry, Joshua at Jericho.

How would I know what to play? I wanted to play a piece my grandmother would recognize. Some klezmer for sure. As August 21 drew near, I practiced every day. I marked my best reed with two stars, the alternate with one. I thought about the distant people who filed into the synagogue when I'd played the "Heyser Bulgar" some years before and added that song to my playlist. I heard my mother saying, "The history of our Jewish people is in that music."

What would my grandmother think if she looked out of the window and saw a crowd of people on the street in front of her apartment, one digging up the bricks to plant a bronze marker? What would she think if she knew her grandson was downstairs? I wondered if my father would have gone with me if he were still alive. I wished he could have.

I emailed David and Frau Krenn that I was coming to Leipzig on August 21. David said if he could get an inexpensive flight from Budapest, he might join me. Achim Beier said he was glad that I was coming, and Frau Krenn sent me the schedule of synagogue services.

Meanwhile, my clarinet looked old and dull. I polished its silvered keys to get it ready for its performance at the Stolperstein ceremony. I was reminded of the story of the genie in a bottle, how rubbing the flask freed the captured spirit within. I wasn't sure if it was more my spirit or my grandmother's that would be freed when I played for her.

♦

I arrived in Leipzig on Thursday afternoon, August

20, by train from Berlin and met Frau Krenn for coffee near her office at the synagogue.

"Are you going to speak at the ceremony tomorrow?" she asked.

I didn't think to say I had brought my clarinet, and I was going to speak through my music.

"Well...no... I wasn't planning to say anything."

"You know, it is rare that a member of the family comes to these services. It would be nice if you could say something."

My first reaction was, *No. In German? You've got to be kidding.*

"I'll see.... Maybe I'll try."

"I would like to be there," Frau Krenn said. "The ceremonies are usually very nice, but I'm sorry I won't be able to attend. My husband and I are leaving on vacation this evening."

We parted after coffee. I wished her a good trip. In the background, my brain was already thinking of what to say at the ceremony. But I didn't know to whom I'd be speaking or how I would deliver the speech in German, or how many people would be there, or what the ceremony would be like, or where I would be standing, or if anyone would even show up, or if hecklers would come by, or if...

Finally, I figured it really didn't matter. I told the panicking ten-year-old inside me not to worry. It would all work out. How many opportunities would I have to speak at the closest thing there would ever be to my grandmother's funeral? And besides, I had made this trip at the boy's insistence, the boy who watched his father cry over his grandmother's picture. He was going to have to sit back and listen to what I had to say, if only I could think of what that would be.

I walked to my grandmother's apartment on the streets I remembered from my last visit. I stood in front of her house for a few minutes, trying to imagine what the scene would look like at noon the next day, during the dedication of the Stolperstein. Unseasonable heat had kept the local pedestrians off the streets, and I was alone. Speaking to no one would probably be easy, I thought.

I walked toward my father's old school and went into the park where he had played soccer more than eighty years before with his rag soccer ball. I called my brother in Wisconsin to share the moment with him. I told him where I was standing and tried to sketch a word-picture for him of what I saw and what I heard. He knew my father's stories, and although they hadn't had the same impact on him as they had on me, we were connected.

"I'm there with you," he said. And then I felt as though he were. I was not so alone.

As I sat on a bench and tried to write what I might say at the ceremony, a couple strolled by, speaking with their child, who was peddling a tricycle. Across the meadow, church bells clanged, and the throbbing air covered the field. Two people disappeared into a black door in the distant trees. A bicycle crunched past on the gravel path, followed by a charcoal dog with a curled tail, his snout low, sniffing the ground.

I wrote down some words. I crossed them out. Who was

I to talk about the Holocaust in Leipzig, Germany, when I lived in comfortable American suburbia? *I* didn't suffer during the Holocaust.

I thought about it for a minute. It wasn't about me. My father had left me some unfinished business to take care of. He had to drop everything and run for his life. I was here to return my grandmother her good name. Max had saved it for all these years in his old suitcase. I was here to say for us, Malka Bein was not forgotten.

Early the next morning I attended the prayer service in the same synagogue my father attended so long ago. I prayed with the same Russian congregation as I had on Kristallnacht, 2008. Grisha recognized me. I explained to him in bits of English, Hebrew, charades, and two German words that I was here for the ceremony for my grandmother that was scheduled for twelve noon. He understood the words *Stolperstein* and *Großmutter*.

"What was her name?" he asked.

"Malka Bein," I said.

He smiled and repeated, "Malka Bein."

I liked the sound. Those words opened a door. They greeted my grandmother, who had been away for seventy years.

◆

I wanted to thank the synagogue congregation for the hospitality they had extended to me on my last visit. They had taken me to the cemetery to see my grandfather's grave, and they shared with me their Sabbath lunch and dinner. I remembered how the head of the congregation had brought back a bottle of Scotch with him after visiting his hometown in Russia. At the community dinner table, he raised the bottle for all to see. They responded with oohs and aahs.

I remembered how they poured it. Everyone shared in a toast at Sabbath dinner. We all raised our glasses and waited for the leader of the community to say the benediction before we drank.

So, I brought with me a bottle of Scotch that I had purchased at the duty-free store in the airport. I wanted the congregation to be able to enjoy a l'chaim, a toast to life, after the Friday night service.

I handed Grisha the bottle.

"For Kiddush?" he asked.

I nodded.

"Tonight?"

I had some difficulty communicating to Grisha that I wasn't going to be able join them in the evening, but they should go ahead anyway.

"Wisout you? Drink wisout you? No," Grisha said.

I didn't know what to do. I wasn't about to take that bottle back to Atlanta with me. I ordinarily didn't drink Scotch at 9 a.m., but that was no ordinary day.

I said, "We drink now? Okay?"

"Okay," he said. "We drink now."

In a couple of minutes, two men emerged from a back room and set in front of me a small table covered with shot glasses. The congregation gathered around. Grisha handed me the bottle and motioned for me to open it. I started pouring. After filling about twenty glasses I got the *stop* signal. I handed the leader of the congregation the first glass and the others helped themselves. He raised his glass and said the blessing, and we toasted to the memory of my grandmother—in her synagogue. She had been in this same place more than seventy years before, but didn't have the chance to say goodbye. I gazed up into the empty balcony where the women sat. I wished I had my clarinet. We could have spoken.

More Scotch was poured. More toasts were made. It was about 9:30 a.m. in Leipzig, but my head said 3:30 a.m., Atlanta. Some of me was still asleep, and the Scotch wasn't helping me get ready for the dedication in a few hours. Showing up drunk would not have been the thing to do. I checked my watch. David's train would be arriving at the Hauptbahnhof in twenty minutes, and I wanted to meet him. I got Grisha's attention, and I pointed to my watch.

I said, "No more for me."

"Why?"

"I'm meeting a friend at the Hauptbahnhof."

I shook everyone's hand and found the door leading out of the synagogue.

In about ten minutes I was back in the train station that had sparked so much memory. The walk cleared my head. I checked the arrival board and found that the Berlin train had already come in, so I walked to the track to meet David.

I stood where the nose of the Berlin train looked into the station. I watched the travelers make their way; some scurrying, some pulling suitcases, some pulling children, some strolling. I scanned the crowd pouring from the passenger cars. Then, halfway down the platform, I saw a waving arm. It was David.

In a few moments he had woven his way through the crowd.

"Nice to see you again. Welcome to Leipzig," I said. I gave him a hug.

"How was your trip?" he asked as we walked out of the Main Hall of the station. It was as if we had been together just yesterday.

The sky was clouding over as we walked back to the hotel to get my clarinet.

"You have to do me a favor," I said. "I've decided, kind of at the last moment, to say a few words at the ceremony at twelve o'clock. Can you translate something for me?"

"Okay, let's sit outside and get a coffee."

We found an empty table at a café, and I pulled out a little spiral notebook with ten hastily scrawled lines that I had written while sitting on the steps of my father's school. The sky was growing darker, and it was going on eleven o'clock. The waitress came. David lit a cigarette and ordered.

"Ich werde einen Kaffee bitte haben."

She turned to me, but I didn't want anything. I just wanted to get my speech translated. I'd have to rewrite it phonetically in German and practice once or twice. Then we needed time to walk over to the house, and I certainly didn't want to be late. I felt anxious about having the time and the place to get warmed up before playing a song on the clarinet for my grandmother. The schedule said twelve, but it didn't really say what was going to happen at twelve, other than I assumed Gunter would put the stone in the ground. I didn't know if I would be able to speak or play, but I was going to try to do both.

The process was the Aurora Café in reverse. This time I read him English, he translated it to German, read it back to me, and I rewrote the words phonetically. As I practiced aloud, the fellow sitting at the next table, smoking a cigarette and drinking coffee, offered some unsolicited but helpful advice. We didn't know how to say, "She left the world without leaving a footprint," and he too had difficulty translating the word footprint. It must have had a different connotation in German.

He offered, "Why don't you say: 'She left the world as if she never lived here?'"

When I said in German that my father left his house forever in 1938, he corrected me and said, "He was forced to leave his house forever."

At eleven-thirty, after my second, reasonable-sounding practice round, the man at the next table rose and said, "Cheers," and disappeared down the street into what was now a pouring rain.

"David, ask for the bill. We've got to go now," I said. "We'll need umbrellas for the walk over there. Maybe we can get some in the train station."

Time was getting short. Luckily, we quickly found an umbrella store, without having to traipse through the largest train station in Europe. On the walk to the house, I kept saying to the black sky, "It can't possibly rain when I've come all this way to stand under my grandmother's window and play a song for her."

David was having trouble keeping a cigarette lit in

the wind and the rain, and when we turned down Uferstrasse there was not a soul in front of the house. That turned out to be a good thing because we were able to stand in the doorway, close our umbrellas, and get out of the rain.

A small crowd soon formed. Grisha and three men from the synagogue arrived under umbrellas and stood in the background. I nodded to them and smiled. They nodded back. I was surprised to see them. Then David pointed to a van across the street with the words Mitteldeutch Rundfunk written across its side.

"German television is here," he said.

More people arrived under umbrellas. Then a group appeared, all with white name tags on their shirts. David spoke with them in German.

"They're from the Leipzig Stolperstein organization," he told me. They will read a short biography of your grandmother, and then they'll introduce you, and you'll read your piece."

A red van pulled up, and Gunter Demnig emerged wearing his signature wide-brimmed hat. Gunter moved as if he wanted to get to work. He was holding the Stolperstein and was met by one of the name-tagged people, who pointed to me. He came over and showed me the stone. I held it in my hand, posing with Gunter in front of the television camera. He was certainly more comfortable in front of the camera's eye than I.

David said, "Seven o'clock news."

I needed the laugh. Time was speeding up, or was not really there at all. I don't remember seeing anyone's face after that, as if I was wearing a hat with the brim pulled down low. The Stolperstein was beautiful. Hammered into the shimmering brass were the German words and my grandmother's name:

Here lived
MALKA BEIN
born 1886
Deported to Poland 28.10.1938
Murdered in Belzyce 1942

When I held the stone in my hand, I thought about the heart surgeons who, during the operation, hold a human heart in their hands.

Traffic was slowing in front of the house. Drivers were looking to see what was going on while Gunter was on his knees dislodging some small stones with a trowel in the entranceway to my grandmother's house. I had to breathe to live, but at that moment, mostly to keep from crying. Gunter was scooping dry cement from a bucket into the space between the stone and the hole in the sidewalk. He took a green plastic watering can and poured its contents onto the stone and the cement. Then he scrubbed the surface of the stone with a hard brush. I was still looking down at it when I heard the story of my grandmother, being read in German. Someone nudged me over, closer to the reader who was handed a portable microphone. I looked for my notes on the torn page of paper that I had stuffed into my pocket when David and I left the café. The reader finished and there was silence.

Gunter was finished. He had returned my grandmother's name to her, and it was there for all to see. She had a marker on this earth. Someone had told me before my trip that every brick in Germany was drenched with Jewish blood. Now there would be fewer of those bricks.

The reader let the sadness of her words hang in the air for a moment before she introduced me. The next few moments were like my wedding day, a blur. I opened up a door to a roomful of people I didn't know, and my nerves rushed in. I don't remember exactly what came next.

The speaker handed me the microphone. I read my German words slowly, not making eye contact with the crowd. I needed all my attention right there on the page. What was I doing reading German, anyway?

I introduced myself and said a bit about my father—that he had worked nearby, went to school in the neighborhood, and prayed at the nearby synagogue until he was forced to leave forever in 1938. I said that my grandmother was killed in a concentration camp and that her bones were scattered in a field somewhere. She never had a funeral. She left the world as if she had never lived here, but now, this stone at her house showed her name for all to see. I stopped reading. I was done.

A hand came in front of me. I put the microphone into it. I didn't know what to do then. It was time to play a song for Malka, but I was so nervous. Would everyone think I was crazy for playing music at a memorial service?

I moved in molasses toward my clarinet case. I had

thought about the moment, written about the moment, and dreamed about the moment, but now that I felt myself in the spotlight, I wished I could be somewhere else. I put my clarinet together and read a note in the case that I had written to myself about which reed to take and which songs to play. I had correctly anticipated being in a fog, just not with such an extreme case of what I can only explain as stage fright.

The rain had stopped. I went into the street, and with my back towards the crowd I played a few quick scales, not much of a warmup. Then I turned and faced my grandmother's house. I looked up at her window and began to play a song by heart. Now I know better what that expression means.

I played songs for her that I thought she might know. The first song was "Eshet Chayil," "A Woman of Valor." Its words are attributed to Abraham, who composed the hymn as a eulogy for his wife Sarah. I played the melody as loudly as I could three or four times with the hope that the music would reach my grandmother, wherever she was.

I wanted to yell up to her window, "Are you there, Grandmother?" But I didn't want the well-behaved Germans assembled on the sidewalk to think I was a nut. Then I played an old Yiddish song, "Oifen Pripitchik," "By the Hearth," and my favorite, "The Heyser Bulgar." I looked for the gray people, the prisoners who came when I played that tune in the synagogue in Columbus. They didn't show up. Maybe I had set them free.

The crowd was thinning. A Stolperstein ceremony was scheduled shortly at another location in Leipzig. I played a few more songs, then put away my clarinet. I was afraid that after playing under my grandmother's window, I wouldn't have the urge or the reason to ever play the clarinet again.

Why would I?

♦

David and I walked away from my grandmother's house. It had all happened so quickly, but I wanted that moment to go on. I turned around. The house looked the same. The road was empty. I walked backwards up the street to keep up with David and keep an eye on the house at the same time. I had thought there would be a difference, that something would have changed. Some years would pass before I realized it was me.

♦

And I thought I was through with that place. I had prayed in my father's synagogue and walked the same streets he had. I stood in the field where he played soccer eighty years earlier, went to his school and to the place where he had worked. I stood under my grandmother's window and played the clarinet for her, and I had left my tears on the sidewalk. But I still needed one more look at the house.

The following day I walked through the train station on the way to my grandmother's apartment and stopped in a bakery for a snack to eat on the way. Germans make wonderful bread. I passed the pretzels, the rolls, the donuts and the croissants, when my attention was drawn to a familiar color and shape, *Pflaumenkuchen*, plum cake.

In 1941, shortly after my immigrant father married my mother, he bought her a German cookbook, *The Settlement Cookbook*. My mother, who liked to cook and was very good at it, got a little tutoring from my father in one special recipe. He liked plum cake and they tweaked the instructions in the book, until after a few trials, he was able to say, "*This* is like my mother used to make."

Every summer when those special plums were in season, my mother made Pflaumenkuchen for my father, and every time he ate it he was careful to say, "This, is like my mother used to make."

So, I bought a piece of Pflaumenkuchen in the train station to eat on the way to my grandmother's house. I appreciate the taste of food and all else good that goes with eating, but until that moment nothing I had ever eaten had made me cry. It *was* like my mother used to make. To hide my tears, I had to gobble down the cake with my back to the Leipzig commuters, hurrying to their trains.

Ten minutes later I was at the house. The street looked the same as it had before. The small brass square quietly occupied its place in the entranceway. The street, with its uneven sidewalk made of granite slabs, some broken, some sloping at odd angles, looked the same. I kneeled and wiped the polished, brass plate clean with my hand. It called out my grandmother's name. I stood nearby for a few moments and watched the passers-by. None looked down. None saw the stone. I wanted to stop them and tell them my story. I wanted to tell them about the shield that shines like gold. "Here lived Malka Bein," it said.

I was going to tell them how I wanted to talk to my grandmother and about my speech in the harsh German language, but that the words had gotten in the way. And then my clarinet had become my voice. I felt like yelling, "FINALLY, I TALKED TO MY GRANDMOTHER."

It was time to go, but I needed some help in cutting myself away from that spot on the earth that had pulled me so close. It now had a marker—a belly button, a center of gravity. It didn't need me.

I turned and walked towards the corner, resisting the urge to turn around and run back. I fought to just keep going. I thought I was through with this place.

Chapter 21

The Sycamore

But I wasn't quite through with this place, because as I stood across the street from my grandmother's apartment, I heard my father's voice in my ears. It was a story he had told me when I was a boy, about his last days in Germany.

"I was walking down my street on the way home from work and saw a police car in front of my house," he said. "It was the Gestapo. I was afraid to go inside, so I waited across the street. After the police had gone in, I rang my doorbell three times, a signal to my mother that I was outside. Then I went back across the street and hid. A short time later the police came out with my mother. She was carrying a small suitcase. They put her in the police car and drove off. That was the last time I saw her."

I got chills when I realized that I was standing in the same place where my father had last seen my grandmother.

But where did he hide?

On this side of the street, there was just another row of houses, shoulder to shoulder, with a bare sidewalk out front. There was no place to hide. Then I saw a tree, just about twenty yards to my right, perhaps five or six stories tall. Its trunk was about four feet in diameter. I measured it, roughly, twelve feet around, certainly large enough for a man to hide behind. Its bark, peeling in blotches of pistachio green and brown, and its spiky seed pods gave it its unmistakable identity. It was a sycamore, with a life span of up to three hundred years. My father must have hidden behind that giant of a tree seventy years ago.

I looked up and down the street to see if anyone was watching.

Then I approached the tree and pressed my hand high up on its trunk, like putting an arm around the shoulder of an old friend. I whispered, "What do you know? What have you seen?" I kept my hand on its rough torso and listened. We were quiet. The tree had seen many things. It had seen the police take my grandmother that day.

"Thank you for hiding my father," I said.

It didn't answer. I guess trees can be like that.

♦

We had similar trees in my Brooklyn neighborhood. I wondered if somehow that familiar look, the mottled skin of the trunk, subconsciously played into my father's choosing where to live after he immigrated to the United States, to New York City, to Brooklyn, and to my street where the sycamores grew.

◆

A detail of the story about my grandmother and my father's hiding place that pains me is of course her abduction by the police. But I can't let go of not knowing if their eyes met, even for an instant, as my grandmother came out of her house with the police on that day. When she looked down Uferstrasse for the last time, did she see my father hiding across the street?

A bit of research told me that the day my father spoke of was October 28, 1938, when approximately 12,000 Polish Jews living in Germany were deported by the nazis to Poland. They were given an hour to pack a suitcase, then taken to the local train stations, jammed into cattle cars, and dumped at the border in the vicinity of the Polish town of Zbaszyn. German soldiers had to fire shots over the heads of the refugees to make them cross over into Poland.

From Zbaszyn, I assume my grandmother was able to afford a seat on the train back to her hometown and her family in Gorlice, even though Jews were only allowed to take ten Marks out of Germany. Surprisingly, my grandmother did not mention the deportation in her letters, or maybe the censor did his dirty job. She only said that no matter what you owned the day before, on October 28, "We all became poor in an hour."

◆

Sycamores propagate through their seed pods, and if I had one I could have planted its seeds and grown a sycamore tree in my yard. I could have had a child of the tree that hid my father from the police so many years ago.

To start the seeds, I would have dried the pod and separated them from the tufts of brown cottonlike material that cushioned and nourished the seeds inside their prickly husk. Then I would have scooped the best fertile soil from my garden into some flowerpots and pressed the seeds into the soil, maybe covering the top with some soft peat. I'd cover the pots that held the seeds with some chicken wire to keep out the hungry birds and squirrels looking for a winter snack. The seeds would need to spend a winter in the cold soil before they germinated.

I would have looked at the flowerpots every day from fall till spring to watch for little peeping green heads pushing through the soil. The day I would have seen a green shoot in those pots would have been a holiday.

I would have waited a bit and transplanted the seedlings into the best soil and sunniest spots in my garden. For that sycamore, I would have given up my vegetable garden, where I worked each year preparing the earth for my tomatoes, peppers, and eggplants. I would have given it all to the child of the sycamore that hid my father.

And after the sycamore had grown a bit I would have felt awful if some rowdy neighbor's kid sneaked into my yard some night when the dog was asleep and scratched his initials into the sycamore's skin with a cheap pocketknife or the edge of a broken beer bottle— or carved a heart around two sets of initials that would last forever and become crusty in the distinctive bark, over which the sycamore would grow a scab.

When I got old, I could sit under the sycamore with my grandchildren and tell them the story of the tree. I'd tell them how the tree's mother hid my father and saved him so many years before, and that we were here today because of the sycamore.

What of my children and their husbands and wives? Would they really care about the tree and the story that some crazy, old gray-haired man told them?

"Poppa, it's just a tree," one of my grown seed pods might tell me.

Certainly, I'd build something with the wood, something to last forever. Maybe I'd make toys for my grandchildren, brightly painted toys with smooth rounded edges. Perhaps I'd make a table.

Maybe a seedling would take a liking to Grandpa's table, not because he or she even knew the story, but just understood from being around Grandpa that the table was special. I could sit in the quiet with my palms pressed flat on its wooden surface and listen again to what its mother saw on October 28, 1938.

Perhaps I'd make a musical instrument from the wood. Its notes would not drop to the earth the way the seed pod that gave it life did, but would fly off towards heaven with a message from the spirits that lived in the wood.

♦

I spied a little Sputnik on a green string, hanging from a branch over my father's street in a place that was just out of my reach. The lower branches would have been easier targets, but they offered none of the spiky pods. I could have used something to stand on, but there were no crates or boxes on the street. I thought of standing on my knapsack for that extra little reach, but that would have drawn attention to something I was trying to do surreptitiously. I stretched for the pod; it was just inches from my fingers, but the stares of the drivers waiting in line at the red light just fifteen feet away made me drop my hand. Imagine going to jail in Germany for stealing state property, a seed pod. I could hear the sing-song wailing siren in the distance, the kind used by German police to make the populace think the Gestapo was on the way. I waited till the street cleared of traffic and was about to snare my catch when a bicycle rider appeared out of nowhere and made me retreat.

I walked away from my quarry, went to the corner, and waited for the light to change and flush away a row of motorized onlookers. As I lingered, more potential eyewitnesses began piling up at the light one by one, putting ogling drivers by my mark. I waited.

I did swipe a seed pod from the sycamore tree that hid my father, and I imagined raising its seedlings in my garden. I took the pod through customs and into the United States without causing an agricultural disaster for importing the likes of the Mediterranean fruit fly. I tried to fool the seeds into thinking they were wintering in Germany by hiding them in the cold and dark of a refrigerator. I thought that a sycamore seed might put forth a green sprout after spending a faux season in a pot of chilly soil, in a white plastic container that had last held vanilla yogurt.

But somehow, that sliver of sycamore memory I had separated from the fluff of its pod knew that it was in a refrigerator in Atlanta, Georgia. It did not flourish.

I should have known better than to force something to grow by hiding it in the dark.

Part III

The Room with the Betampte Kitchen

Chapter 22

The Bubble

A few years after translating my grandmother's letters, I was a chaperone for a group of two hundred high school students on a "roots" trip to Poland. We spent a week tracing our ancestors' steps through the cities and towns where they lived and the concentration camps where many of them died. It is said that four out of five American Jews can trace their roots to Poland.

I knew it would be a difficult trip when I learned there would be armed guards on our buses. Previous youth trips had encountered hostility from some locals. We couldn't imagine how a community remained oblivious during the war years to a concentration camp, a killing factory, literally down the street. Maybe they couldn't imagine why we kept showing up every year in their streets, carrying signs, singing songs, and waving flags.

Our burly guards, young Polish men hired by the trip organizers, told us, "We make bubble around you. Don't go outside bubble," their beefy arms miming the not-so-worldly sphere.

I knew it would be difficult when I found out we would travel with social workers. Our instructions said, "Don't let anyone walk by themselves in the camps. Too dangerous. Too depressing. I tried to prepare myself by watching *Schindler's List*. I couldn't sit through it.

Our trip was going to take us to Krakow, connected on the map to Gorlice by a two-inch, blood-red capillary. Gorlice was the return address of the letters that lived in my father's suitcase. I would be so close, but our instructions were: No side trips. Stay with the group. No exceptions.

I felt the tug of my ancestors and knew that I would feel them more strongly in Poland, but I had to live on that leash. "The trip is for the kids, not their guides," the organizers said.

♦

The clothes in my duffle bag crowded out the things I wanted to take. It made me think of my father, packing a lifetime into his suitcase on Kristallnacht. How difficult that must have been. I thought of my grandmother, given an hour to pack her bag before the police took her to the train station and deported her to Poland.

I found a safe spot in my bag for the picture of my grandmother wearing her stylish black hat with the broad brim and the dark dress that reached down to the tops of her polished black shoes. That picture may have been taken in Gorlice, before she left for Germany in the early 1900s. It was the picture my father showed me when I was ten, when his voice became small and strange, when he said, "This is your grandmother," and I asked, "Where is she?"

I took a picture of the page in my father's passport with the red crayon scrawled JID, JEW, written in 1938 at the Czechoslovakian border. I took a letter sent in 1940 by my grandmother in Gorlice to my father in New York City. It was stamped Censored and Geöffnet [opened] next to the mark of the German eagle and swastika.

I wanted to take my clarinet to play klezmer to the spirits in the concentration camps. Poland birthed klezmer music, but I didn't know if klezmer, Jewish wedding music, in such a place would be disrespectful. Those souls had missed so many weddings.

There was certainly enough room in my bag for the yarmulke that a neighbor, Rose, had knitted for me. She was a sweet lady from somewhere in Poland with a history knotted in the Holocaust. Rose was like everyone's grandma, though I could only imagine what a grandmother would be like; and we were her grandchildren. She had died a few years earlier and had a son somewhere. I wanted to take her yarmulke to Poland.

♦

Shabbos in Krakow we went to synagogue. I was scared. This was Poland and we were Jews. I spent some time during the service trying to find the right prayer book on the shelves that held books in ten foreign languages, but more time looking at the names on the memorial plaques on the wall. Krakow was not far from Gorlice, and I thought maybe I could find a family name on one of those commemorative metal plates.

After services I was invited to the rabbi's house for lunch. We walked through the city in a group with an armed guard, but the rabbis, wearing their tallisim, prayer shawls, led the way. I felt like a target, fortunately only of stares. At the rabbi's apartment, the guard stood outside the door of the second floor flat and waited hours to escort us back after lunch.

The rabbi's few small rooms were an oasis for Jewish travelers. We waited for him in his living room mingling with his other guests. I met a middle-aged woman who told me she was from New York, Crown Heights to be exact. I told her I was from Brooklyn and now lived in Atlanta.

"Atlanta," she said. "I had an old aunt who lived in Atlanta. She died many years ago."

"What was her name?" I asked.

The woman squinted and looked upward. She thought for a moment.

"Rose. Rose Rabinowitz."

I got goosebumps.

I bent my head toward her and said, "See this yarmulke I'm wearing? Rose Rabinowitz made this yarmulke for me. I wore it for her because she came from Poland."

The woman gasped. "Oy, I'm getting shivers." She began to rub her skin. Then she waved her arms as if she was flagging down the last car leaving the planet. She yelled across the room, "Meyer, Meyer," and pointed to a man with a white beard and a black hat. He came our way.

"That's my brother," the woman said to me. She poked the air with a finger. "Tell him the story. Tell him the story."

So I told Meyer about the yarmulke. He rubbed his arms too.

"But wait a second," he said. "How do I know that the woman who made your yarmulke is really my aunt?"

"That's a good question," I said. For a moment, I doubted the coincidence myself.

"Rose worked for the phone company," I told him.

Meyer slapped his hands together. "That's her, that's Rose. She *did* work for the phone company."

I asked Meyer, "What brings you from Crown Heights in Brooklyn to the rabbi's table in Krakow?"

"We were on our way to Gorlice and it was getting too close to Shabbos to travel, so we came here. We'll go Sunday."

"*Gorlice.* My family is from Gorlice. My grandmother and her family lived there before the war. I'll show you her picture."

Meyer said, "My grandfather was the rabbi of Gorlice before the war."

"I have an old book, and there is a picture of your grandfather there, I said. "I can send it to you when I get home."

We tried to remember each other's phone numbers, but it was Shabbos, and we couldn't write them down. Meyer changed the numbers of my phone number into letters of the alphabet, Hebrew words in his head. We agreed that the most difficult part had already happened. If we were to meet like this, then connecting the second time would not be a problem.

Then Meyer said, "I want you to come with us. We're going to Gorlice tomorrow."

I thought I was dreaming. I wouldn't have believed it if I saw it in the movies.

"I can't. I have to stay with the trip. And besides, I'm not ready to go to Gorlice."

"What's there to get ready for? You can come with us and go back and meet up with your trip the next day."

"No," I told him. "I have to stay with the trip," while in the back of my mind I imagined what my trip mates would say if I wasn't on the bus in the morning.

I felt like I was standing on the edge of a rooftop, and I could fly, if I jumped. Only I couldn't jump.

Chapter 23

Tesknie Za Toba Zydzi
(I Miss You, Jews)

I invited my grandmother to my son's high school graduation; the school provided the invites. I printed *Malka Bein, Piekarska 2, Gorlice, Poland* on the envelope, the return address on the letters that lived in my father's suitcase. I licked the back of the airmail stamp and stuck it in the corner of the envelope.

"Good luck," I said when I dropped it in the mailbox at the post office.

My grandmother didn't reply. I waited. And waited.

I began to worry.

It wasn't like her not to answer me. How could she have ignored my invitation? Maybe she hadn't seen it. Maybe she hadn't seen it because she hadn't been home in so long. Where was she? My grandmother had never gone missing before. Could she have just disappeared?

I thought of going to Poland to search for her. It wasn't as if she were a dog who sneaked out the back door and scampered through the open gate when no one was paying attention and then couldn't find her way home again. She was a human. How could my grandmother have been so easily lost and forgotten?

My grandmother had been taken from me, and I wanted her back. I wanted her to know that I had come looking. So, I thought one night I would wake before the sun, pull on my pants, lace up my shoes, and go out to find her and her brothers, my great uncles, Yantsche and Meyer. They were all expected home but didn't return. The ten-year-old inside me wanted to go to Poland to find his grandmother. I was just going along to carry his suitcase.

♦

When 500,000 people didn't come home from Belzec, did anyone miss them? Did anyone notice the quiet emptiness in the market square, or the gray smoke that twisted from a jagged hole in a window of the desolate synagogue? Did anyone notice that the shoemaker's shop wasn't open anymore, or that no one answered when the cows bellowed to be milked?

Who realized that the Shabbos candles weren't lit, and the challah dough sitting in the wooden bowl on the kitchen table had risen as large as a pillow? Who cared that the Yiddish newspaper went unread, folded on the armchair's worn cushion, or that the letters addressed to my grandmother went unopened and lay in a mosaic of envelopes on the floor just inside her front door?

But I was scared to go to Poland, where I was scared to be a Jew. Where almost 4,000,000 Jews had lived in 1939, now, there were in 2010 only thousands. Where there had been hundreds, if not thousands of active Jewish communities and synagogues, there were only two, one in Warsaw and one in Krakow. Almost 25% of the world's Jewish population had lived in Poland in 1939. What had been the cultural, religious, and academic center of Judaism for hundreds of years was now a Jewish wilderness and had been erased in the minds of some from Polish history.

But when the graduation invitation I had mailed to my grandmother came back to me, it took me by surprise. I recognized the envelope and for a flash forgot it had been seventy years since she disappeared. So much excitement packed into the blink of an eye, thinking that she had answered. Could she make it? When would she come? For one second, I thought about sitting next to her at the graduation.

When I examined the envelope carrying the postman's Polish scribble, I came to, but the flash of hope fanned a flame. I didn't know what the scrawl said; maybe "Return to sender" or "Addressee unknown." I would have preferred the former. But I settled for an envelope that had reached Gorlice and returned, wearing a familiar, almost familial seal, the postmark of Gorlice, resembling so many of the stamped faces on the letters in my father's suitcase. That invitation caused me to think of the birds that Noah had sent out from the ark in search of dry land.

I don't know what was changing, but I began to think more seriously about going back to Poland. It certainly would have been easier for me to stay home, and I was frightened about meeting up with history, but some mysterious beam was pulling on me from that crazy place. It was a tug of war, me versus it. I would have to face the Belzec concentration camp, and how could I get ready to do *that*? Belzec, the place where my grandmother was murdered; where the guards slept on mattresses stuffed with human hair; where 500,000 died and not one survived.

♦

I read that some current-day Christian Poles acknowledged a piece missing from their history, and it was a gap they wanted to repair. In their hearts, they felt a hole had been torn in their past when almost four million of their Jewish neighbors were eliminated from Polish society. That piece of their culture, the Jews, who had lived for almost six hundred years in Poland, was gone.

I became interested in a website based in Poland, describing a project called *Tesknie Za Toba Zydzie, I Miss You, Jews*. Its creators intended to collect memories of Jewish people who had disappeared during the war. I imagined that one such memory may have been created when it became trapped inside a camera. It was the echo of a lost Sunday afternoon at the park in 1939

Gorlice. It spilled at the last instant through the slamming shutter, etching a moment on a slick strip of acetate whose perforated edges wound round a spiky spindle. The memory became a prisoner in a miniature metal can, but developed into a smooth stack of twenty-four, three-by-five black-and-whites. All but one displayed the faces of strangers.

So, when I found an entry posted from Gorlice on Tesknie.com, I thought it might hold something of my grandmother: that 1939 picture, a song, her chicken soup, her new scarf. Although I could not get a clear image in my mind from the Polish words that appeared on my computer screen, I thought that the one who had posted the item, the neighbor's child perhaps, knew my grandmother. Maybe they lived in the house next to Piekarska 2 and one afternoon had invited my grandmother for a glass of tea. I could imagine her saying she worried about my father, that he looked so thin in his last picture. Why wasn't he eating?

Maybe the neighbors used to go to the rynek, the market square, with my grandmother when she went on Fridays before Sabbath to buy soup greens and potatoes and a little flour. I itched to know any little detail, anything at all about my grandmother, any memory, perhaps the one the neighbor's child just posted on that website.

To those Polish bits, I added the little that I knew of my grandmother, sending my reflection off to that internet place, hoping that both memories might mingle and create a more vivid image, or a new remembrance, more genuine than the strongest I could summon, perhaps a new living memory.

♦

I felt the pull of that mysterious magnet, reaching from the foothills of the Carpathian Mountains, more than three thousand miles away. I wrestled with the obligation to visit the place where my grandmother's soul took flight. But I still tripped over the horror of Belzec.

I imagined the approach to that horrible place. Where would the darkness begin? Would there be light and then darkness, a high wall with light before it and darkness across its edge? Or would there be gradations in the shading of light and darkness? Would the wall offer some resistance and coat those who passed through it, giving them another skin?

Would the darkness be like a curtain? The curtain, scalloped in shadows, might let the light and gloom mix through each other in places to my left or right. Or would the darkness mix with the light like smoke, coming on slowly, swirling around me, blowing darker and brighter like a fog?

Where would I shower after going to Belzec? What would I do with my clothes? Could I burn them? Would I ever be able to eat again? What would I do with the dust that collected on my shoes at Belzec? Could I wash it off?

But something inside me said: *This is the time. Go to Poland now. You might not get another chance.* Maybe it was my grandmother speaking.

I listened.

I contacted David in Budapest and asked him if he

had any interest in going to Poland. I told him I was thinking about returning to the place my grandmother's letters had come from, the letters he had translated in Atlanta. I unconsciously used the word "returning." Must have been inherited memory.

He emailed back and said that his family, too, had come from Poland, from a little town called Pulawy, and he might want to visit there as well. The possibility of a trip to Poland was sinking in. That mysterious pull was getting stronger. I could soak up the place where my grandmother had lived. Perhaps I could let my thoughts run free in the synagogue where she had talked to G-d.

◆

My shtetl book became a guidebook to my past. The book has oversized, yellowing pages. The paper is dry and will soon fall from its binding. From a cut up brown paper bag, I made a book cover to protect it. Its Hebrew words are interspersed with black-and-white photos of familiar strangers.

Shtetl means "village" in Yiddish, a village with many Jews. Many shtetls have their own books; mine is from Gorlice. My book is a book of memories, created after the war by former Gorlice residents. It contains their remembrances, in stories, in letters, and in pictures gleaned from survivors who wanted to preserve an essence of their former lives. The book is an annotated graveyard with pictures between a front and back cover. Turning its pages pushes my imagination into the past.

I looked into my old shtetl book that day because I wanted to find my family.

I wished they could come out from behind their 1939 picture taken at the annual Purim party. Lola had written a letter to my father saying that she was in Gorlice during Purim 1939, while visiting my grandmother. She wondered why she didn't see anyone from the family at the party. "Too frum?" she wrote, wondering if they were too religious to attend the wild celebration, commemorating the defeat of the conspirators wishing to exterminate the Jews of ancient Persia.

The Hebrew text in my book made navigation difficult, but the surname index on the last page led me to a 1921 picture of my great-uncle Meyer, Malka's brother. He wore a short dark beard and mustache, suit, tie, and a yarmulke. He was a member of a delegation receiving a visitor to the community. I felt a special connection to great-uncle Meyer because he had sent my father an invitation in 1939 to the wedding of his daughter in Gorlice. That invitation lived in my father's suitcase until I freed it to tell its story. I thought of the page of testimony in Yad Vashem that I found online. It said my uncle Meyer was murdered in Gorlice. Unfortunately, I couldn't warn his 1921 picture of the future. Time messes things up.

The shtetl book had a memory of Malka's parents. It said that Malka's mother, Chia, managed a bakery with her two sisters. Her father, Menashe, was a cantor in the synagogue. The transcribed memory said he would pray for anyone at any time. The story about him having the right to sell cheesecake and schnapps for "L'Chaim" in the synagogue during the week made me chuckle. It said that my great grandfather sang his own special melody during the afternoon prayer on Saturday. I wondered how it sounded. Did I sing the same notes when I prayed?

I was sad to see the paragraph about my family in the shtetl book come to an end. It said the evening before Yom Kippur, Menasche delivered prayer books to congregants' homes and gave honey cake to the children. That was all. A few grains of sand tweezed from a beach. I felt as though the person on the other end of the phone had hung up in the middle of the call.

I wanted to find their synagogue. I thought there might be a picture of it with a street name in the shtetl book, but there was none. Then on the internet, I read about a bakery in current-day Gorlice that had been a synagogue prior to 1939.The bakery was on Piekarska, which looked like a short road on the street map. It had to be near my grandmother's apartment. How many bakeries could there be?

More research told me about a synagogue on Piekarska built in the early 1900s. That was it. How many synagogues could there be on that short street? The old synagogue and the bakery had to be in the same place. Local artisans, it said, had been hired to paint the ceiling, and they decorated it with a scene of two lions holding the Ten Commandments. *I* was going to visit those lions in my grandmother's synagogue.

Then it struck me that I would be going into the

synagogue where my cousin Ida Frauwirt was married on August 25, 1939. I had imagined being there once before, when I met my family moments after reading the wedding invitation that lived in my father's suitcase. Now I would be going there again. I wondered how those two scenes would meet and reconcile, and I understood why I used the word "return" to describe the trip to David.

♦

I would go to that synagogue in Gorlice early in the morning, in time for Shacharis, the morning prayer. I would stand outside and watch the congregants hurrying to the service, carrying their tallisim, their prayer shawls. I'd meet my great uncles, Yantsche and Meyer. They would hug me and clap me on the back, introduce me to their friends with the excitement of boys, not bearded men. I'd sit between them in a long wooden pew, the one near the bimah, the podium, where they always sat. During Kiddush, I'd watched as they dipped their honey cake into the herring bowl. They would point to me to do the same.

After the synagogue service, we walked to Uncle Yantsche's shoemaker's shop, my arm over his shoulder. I watched him kibbitz with customers while he ripped worn heels from their shabby shoes, then painted the glue onto the heelless last with a fat brush from the pot that had grown wide from years of dried drippings – grey, glue stalactites. He glanced at me now and then, sitting in the rear of his shop, out of sight, in the midst of the fragrances of glue and leather.

♦

I sent an email to the genealogical society, JewishGen, asking if anyone had recently been to Gorlice or Belzec. A handful of replies came back. In one of them, Chana Becker in Israel asked if I could look up the names of her family, lost at Belzec. I told her I would. I liked the idea of taking the names of her family with me, so I wouldn't feel so lonely.

Even though I wasn't looking forward to being in Poland, and the guidebook said that there really wasn't any reason for tourists to go to Gorlice, I thought I might stay over for an evening to get a better idea of what it might have been like to live there. Then I could spend more time walking on the same streets as my family had. Gorlice had an inn, a place with four rooms called the Dark Dungeon. But I was hesitant to be a Jew in Gorlice, or a Jew in Warsaw, or a Jew anywhere in Poland. Was I really going to stay in a place called the Dark Dungeon?

I looked at my grandmother's street again on the map. I wanted to walk up one side and down the other, examining every doorpost for the rubbed-out shadows of mezuzah's, traces of the Jews who had once lived there. The map said there was an internet café at Piekarska 6, just down the street. I would take a letter there for David to translate, as we had done at the Aurora in Atlanta; only this time I would be taking the letter back home.

I read a story on the internet written by a man in the 1990s who had returned to Gorlice, his birthplace.

He wrote that he recognized some of the places he knew as a boy. That was good news. The war hadn't been fought there, and the city hadn't been bombed, so I'd be able to see Gorlice the way it looked to my grandmother.

More research took me to another website describing a trip to Gorlice taken by high school students. The story told of how the tour bus stopped at an anonymous spot in the woods outside of town at an unmarked mass grave where the nazis had executed hundreds of Jews during the war. I wondered if great-uncle Meyer was marched off to that place. Did his wife and children watch him go?

♦

I reread my grandmother's letters. She had written one in the spring of 1939, after her deportation to Poland. My grandmother had been living with an aunt in Gorlice, in a room with four other refugees. She was grateful for the roof over her head, but had her fill of the close quarters. My grandmother managed to move into her own apartment and wrote in 1939 that it was a "nice room with a betampte kitchen." I wanted to go to that room with the homey kitchen on Piekarska 2.

I'll wait outside the apartment, maybe across the street. If her Polish neighbors discover my story, will they think me crazy? When will my grandmother come out and walk to the rynek, the market square?

I'll sit in the rynek and wait for her while I look at one of her letters. Maybe an old lady, gray and bent, will come; the old lady who was ten years old on August 14, 1942, when the nazis carted off the Jews of Gorlice.

That would make her seventy-eight years old. Maybe she was a Jewish girl who hid, or passed as Christian because of her blonde braids. Maybe she knew my grandmother. Perhaps she was the one who I'd envisioned rescuing a letter my father wrote; the letter that blew on the summer breeze on August 14 when the mob of drunken slobs looking for Jewish gold tore through the apartments of the Jews who were Dead or soon to be Dead.

Maybe the old lady, wearing a scarf covering her hair, saved the envelope with a letter and a picture of my father, and sees the resemblance in my face while I sit in the rynek in Gorlice. I see out of the corner of my eye the old, bent woman. She digs into the stuffed bag she is carrying, a paper bag inside a plastic one with handles. She comes out with a picture that she holds far enough away for her eyes to focus on a face. She looks at me and looks at the picture, and looks at me again. I get up from my seat and take a step toward her.

"What is it, dear?" I say.

She is frightened, puts the picture away and hobbles off on stiff legs. She is frightened by a familiar face that came out of a picture she rescued seventy years ago.

♦

Again, I thought of my father's story about returning home to Leipzig by train in the late 1930s, coming near to Gorlice, but not visiting his relatives because he didn't have the money to buy them gifts. The Germans invaded shortly thereafter, and he never saw his relatives again. That story, which haunted him for the rest of his life, has taken a hold on my soul.

What gifts can I bring to Gorlice that I could leave behind for my family? Where would I leave them? Maybe I could take the seeds from the sycamore that hid my father in Leipzig and plant them in the Jewish cemetery. But what could I bring for the children and for the newly married couple, my cousins Ida Frauwirt and Moses Moster? But maybe they ran when the nazis came into town. Maybe they began a family somewhere else in the world.

I couldn't think of what to bring to Gorlice, but arriving empty-handed would be better than not arriving at all. It would slay one of my father's demons.

The imagination of that ten-year-old inside me wanted to ride the train between Gorlice and Krakow, as my grandmother had done in 1939. She had to retrieve a parcel sent by my father that was being held in Krakow, she wrote. My imagination also wanted to go to the post office in Gorlice, where my grandmother and her letters had been.

My grandmother wrote about her brother, my great-uncle Mecheul, who lived in a nearby town, Nowy Sacz. He had invited her for Passover in the spring of 1939, and she had spent the holiday with him and his family. That was the uncle my father told me about when I was a boy. Mecheul was so poor or so religious that he fasted twice a week, on the days they read from the Torah in synagogue in Nowy Sacz. I added Nowy Sacz and its synagogue and cemetery to my itinerary, hoping they still existed, and I could find them.

I wanted to retrace my grandmother's 1938 exile, on a railroad from the German border, to Gorlice, so I located an online map of Poland's railroad system. Everything is on the internet. I wanted to ride into the Gorlice train station as she had done after her deportation in 1938. But I learned that the Gorlice station was situated a few kilometers from town. When Malka arrived in Gorlice in 1938 after her exile, her family met her, but they weren't going to meet me. I wouldn't be able to get from the train into the town and Piekarska 2. There was a shuttle bus from the rail station to Gorlice. A website said it ran every few hours, but that didn't sound like a promise, so I didn't want to rely on that bus for a visit to my grandmother and the room with the betampte kitchen.

I thought about how to get to the concentration camp at Belzec. Even though it had been located beside railroad tracks in 1941, the rail map showed there was no current-day connection from Gorlice to Belzec, so making the trip on the memory-laden Polish railroad system was unfortunately not an option. If I wanted to go to Gorlice or Belzec, I'd have to go by car, though I knew I'd be leaving something behind, untouched on the railroad – a glance, a touch, a familiar face I'd never seen.

When I emailed the JewishGen group asking if anyone had been to Gorlice or Belzec, I found out that some had hired drivers. When I received a reference about a driver, Rojan, I wanted to email him about possibly driving David and me on a roots tour. But what would I tell him? "Take me to the ghetto where my grandmother lived, where her brothers were shot on August 14, 1942. Take me to the ghetto where my grandmother and nieces and nephews were rounded up and marched off to the railroad and packed into cattle cars and shipped to the killing factory."

Should I say to him: "My family is Polish, and I am going to visit their house"? It wasn't a house, or even an apartment. It was a room, just a room. I could tell him, "Please take me to the room with the betampte kitchen."

I kept my email to Rojan simple, and he replied some days later. He proposed driving from Warsaw, where he lived and where my plane would land, to Pulawy, Belzec, and Gorlice in about four days. But his fee would have broken the bank. More importantly, I thought the trip for David and me was kind of private, spiritual in a way, and that Rojan's presence might interfere somehow in our rite. I ruled out a driver, but I at least knew that making the trip by car was possible.

I went to the local AAA office in Norcross, Georgia, for some help navigating Poland.

"Is this a pleasure trip?" they asked.

"No, I'm going to Poland. I'm going to Poland."

They didn't understand, but offered to get me a quote on a car, a few nights in a hotel, and a rail trip from Krakow to Warsaw to quench my ten-year-old's imagination. However, when the outrageous quote came back, I figured I should book all the pieces of the trip on the internet myself, car, train, and hotel.

The thought of driving a car through Poland raised goosebumps on my skin. I didn't speak one word of Polish, and I imagined getting stuck on the side of the road with a flat tire. I imagined trying to call for assistance on the Polish cellphone I didn't yet own and explaining the problem without the benefit of being able to act out the tire flatness in charades. But this trip was a once in a lifetime chance, my dream too easily deflated by a flat tire on a rented car.

I could smell the burning clutch of a rental with an unfamiliar manual transmission and could feel my car sliding backwards into the truck behind me after trying to get into gear on a hill near Gorlice, creating an international incident. I saw the truck drivers standing beside the broken glass in the road, caps in hand, pointing at the crunched socket that, once upon a time, held a round headlight.

Reports on the internet of drunken driving in Poland and of Russian gangs coming across the Polish border at night to steal cars kept me awake at night. I read descriptions of an archaic highway system under constant repair, slowed to a crawl by frequent bicycle riders and creeping farm equipment. My goosebumps got goosebumps. The US State Department website said, "Driving, especially after dark, is hazardous."

I hadn't left myself many alternatives for getting around Poland, and I had already purchased a plane ticket. The clock was ticking.

The AAA in Norcross made me an international driver's license on the spot for $25.

"Stand over there against the wall and look at me," the man in the office said from behind one of those cameras that developed its own pictures.

He cut the photo to fit into the gray folder of the

license and filled out the paperwork. But I didn't like my place of birth, Brooklyn, NY, listed on the certificate. Brooklyn was too close an association to being Jewish. It was the home of one million Jews. It seemed crazy, but I didn't want my driver's license to out me as a Jew in Poland.

The driving was bothering me. Being Jewish in Poland was bothering me. This was another trip that would have been easier not to take, and I wasn't meeting anyone who said, "Going to Poland? What a great idea. I'm jealous!"

The script was similar to the responses I had heard a year earlier when I went to Germany.

"You're going where?"

I stopped telling people that I was planning to go to Poland.

But I had to go. I didn't have a choice. I had to go to Piekarska 2 and Nowy Sacz. I had to go to Belzec.

Ever since I opened my father's suitcase that lived at the bottom of his closet, ever since I felt the electricity of my grandmother's letters in my hands and touched with my fingertips the words she had written, I was smitten with the idea of going to Poland. I had to see the place where my grandmother lived and the place where she sat in front of the window behind the parted curtain at the wooden table to write her letters. When I listened closely, I could hear the scratch of the nib of my grandmother's fountain pen as her linked, inked curls flowed out onto the onion-skin paper.

Chapter 24

Finally, a Grandson

My father never knew exactly when his mother died; there were no surviving witnesses. But to mark the calendar, he chose a summer day, near to the time when the Jewish population of Gorlice was hauled off to Belzec. We commemorated that day every year. This year, as I was planning to go to Poland, that day crept closer.

Ten Jewish men make a *minion*, the quorum needed to recite Kaddish, the prayer for the dead. I remember summer vacations in Vermont or in Upstate New York, watching my father seek out synagogues in small towns, walking their Main Streets with him to find the likes of Goldberg's Dry Goods or Katz's Delicatessen. How embarrassed I'd be, watching him cajole gray-haired Jewish men, some of whom hadn't been to synagogue since their bar mitzvahs, into joining a minion so he could pray for his mother on the anniversary of her death. However, there was still no discussion of her life.

As the anniversary approached, and for the first time in my life, I felt deeply connected to that day, as though *I* were entering a period of mourning. I even stopped shaving and grew a beard, a custom of Jewish males mourning for immediate family. I planned to wear the beard until I returned from my trip, though when I thought about going to Belzec:

> I wanted to hide.
> I wanted to be   i   n   v   i   s   i   b   l   e
> And looked for a *disguise.*
>
> I hunted for CamOuflAge
>
> I sought a hat.
> I bought a jacket,
> A cloth skin with sleeves
> But I looked like a **prisoner** in gray.
>
> I grew a ^{b}ear^d
> It too was gray.

Some in synagogue wanted to know why I was growing a beard. They asked politely, because in an Orthodox community a new beard can be the sign of a death in the family. People wanted to be respectful and supportive, but didn't want to stumble into an uncomfortable place.

"Forgot to shave this morning?" or, "I like the beard, any special reason?" they'd say.

I felt embarrassed for being unable to tell them I was growing it to get ready to go to Belzec, Poland. I wasn't able to say I was thinking about my grandmother who was murdered there. I could have said that I *had* suffered a death in the family – seventy years ago. But they would have thought I was crazy.

Through the whiskers I viewed in the mirror, I had created for myself an opportunity to talk about what I felt as I was preparing to visit my grandmother. I created the opportunity to talk about the feeling of mourning for her, but I wasn't comfortable enough to have that conversation with a stranger.

And there were too many strangers.

♦

I had breakfast with a friend. We had been meeting in the same restaurant on and off for years. As I approached his table he looked up from his writing and stood.

"Hello friend," he said. "It's been a while."

"I can't remember the last time."

We gave each other a loose hug. He pulled back a few inches and eyed me closely, like an old person trying to read a book without his glasses.

"I like the beard," he said, and put a hand to his face to stroke some imaginary stubble.

"Thanks."

"I had a beard when I went to college. Yours looks good. Maybe I'll grow one again."

We sat down, and I told him I was planning to go to Gorlice.

"I did some research. The old synagogue across the street from my grandmother's apartment is a bread factory now. When it was built in the early 1900s the community hired local artisans to paint the interior, and they decorated the ceiling with a painting of two lions holding the Ten Commandments. I want to get inside the factory and see that ceiling."

"Do any Jews still live there?"

"No, I don't think so. They were all killed or driven away. I've heard stories about some who came back to their hometowns after the war – concentration camp survivors. When they returned to their former houses some found them occupied by old neighbors, and they were not welcomed back. I'm a little fearful about going."

"When did we start meeting for breakfast?" my friend asked.

I thought for a moment. "About eight years ago."

"We haven't seen each other in a while, but I remember that you talked about this trip way back then. You weren't ready to go. You were scared, even then."

He mimed a shaking motion with his hands, as if in fear. "You told me about going to the place where your grandmother died. Tell me again, what's it called?"

"Belzec."

"You described the place as being in a large field beside a forest."

"The nazis razed the concentration camp in 1943, but they wanted to hide what they had done, so they established a farm over an unmarked cemetery of five or six hundred thousand dead. They made a camp guard the farmer."

My friend grimaced.

"I've wanted to write a poem about the people who ate the vegetables that grew on that farm. Not exactly peppermint mocha with whip," I said. "The Germans tore up the railroad tracks that took the prisoners to the camp and they planted a forest."

"We had been meeting here almost every other week for a few years," my friend said. After the first time you told me that story I pictured that forest every time I thought of you." He closed his eyes, far away, his head tilted upward. "It's a pine forest, and it's symmetric."

I shrugged. "I'll find out soon."

"Will you bring back a little bag of dirt?" he asked.

"*A bag of dirt?*" I shot upright in my chair. The thought made my teeth hurt.

"As a remembrance."

"Definitely not. The nazis ground up the bodies of the people they murdered, trying to hide the evidence. There are pieces of bones in the earth. It's a cemetery."

I sat back in my chair again. He changed the topic.

"Where else will you go?"

"I want to go to my grandmother's apartment in Gorlice. The place is still there. I saw it on the internet. It looks like a store."

He stared out the window into the parking lot for a moment. Then he turned towards me.

"I'm going to ask you something that may be totally inappropriate. You tell me if it is."

"Okay," I said. "Ask."

"What kind of store is it?"

"I'm not sure, tobacco maybe."

He reached into his back pocket and took out his wallet.

"Are you going to buy anything there?"

"I don't know. Probably not."

I didn't tell him that I was going to find the place repulsive. I wouldn't be a tourist, and I didn't want a souvenir.

"I'm going to give you ten dollars. I'd like you to buy me something in that tobacco store – a cigar, whatever. You've told me about the letters and this trip for so long. That cigar, or whatever it is, will anchor our relationship. I'm going to put it on my shelf. It's a link to your grandmother."

I shook my head. "Let's do this instead. Hold onto the ten dollars. If I decide to buy something in that store, I'll ask you for the money back."

"Fair enough."

After breakfast I drove to synagogue in Atlanta. The rabbi was in the office, and Adrienne, the office secretary, was sitting at her desk. The chair, next to the rabbi's desk, was occupied by his black hat. It was like another person. I chuckled to myself and wondered if the rabbi had to buy two seats on airplanes, one for him and one for his hat. I didn't ask.

"I like your beard," the rabbi said. "It's artistic. How long are you going to keep it?"

"Probably till I get back from Poland."

"When are you going?"

"August second, and my grandmother's yahrzeit is coming up soon. I came here today because I want to give the synagogue library a book in her honor."

Adrienne said, "That's a nice memory for your family. What would you like the dedication to say?"

I shrugged.

"We don't know your grandmother's name." She tore a sheet of yellow paper from a legal pad. "What was it?"

"Malka, Malka Bein."

She wrote carefully on the paper, "In commemoration of the yahrzeit of Malka Bein, from her grandson Peter Bein."

I liked being Malka's grandson. I had never been called that.

Never.

And at that moment, in the Hollywood movie in my mind, trumpets blared.

♦

From the synagogue office, I went to the supermarket and bought two little yahrzeit lamps, memorial candles that I wanted to light at the Belzec concentration camp. I wanted to light one lamp for Malka and one lamp for everyone else whose bones lay under the ground. I bought the metal lamps, little cans of wax, rather than the glass kind. The metal would be easier to carry and survive the trip in a crowded duffle bag better than glass. David was a smoker, so I was guaranteed to be around matches.

I wanted the light from the candles to radiate and not to be cooped up in that tiny metal can. I wanted the skyward-pointing flame to be visible to all those looking down from the heavens onto Belzec. I wanted Malka's candle to burn at night in the midst of the darkness that sits always on Belzec like a smothering weight. Even in the day, I thought the darkness would be over that place like an eclipse.

I wondered: Would there be other people walking around Belzec? Religious Jews in black hats, nonreligious Jews in street clothes, Gentiles? Would we talk? What would we say? What are you doing here? Do you come here often? I could only think of inappropriate things to say to other people I might meet at Belzec, so I decided I wouldn't be comfortable talking to anyone once I got there.

Any person at Belzec would be made from a strange material that reacted to the pull of the crazy magnet that drew us from our warm beds, propelled us on a difficult path, and compelled us for a reason we didn't quite understand. The path crossed over mountains and forests, cities and water and rose into the sky so high that the air became near-frozen, so thin that it wasn't really air anymore. So high that at night, we approached the stars. We continued on a train, in a borrowed car, on a ribbon of road that curled through villages and neat green fields to a place where half of a forest met half of a farm planted on top of shattered human bones. Such a strange farm. What grew there?

Would I want to get out of the safety of the enclosure of a car to be alone with nothing between me and that horrible place?

I debated bringing my clarinet to Belzec. I wanted to play for my grandmother as I had done for her in Leipzig, for her Stolperstein ceremony. I wanted to play for all those who had lost a soul and I wanted to play for all those under the earth, but I didn't know if it would be appropriate. To some, Belzec was a cemetery. I felt that as well, but I could go off into the woods and play a melody that would cut through the darkness, wafting over the stones to cover the bones of Malka and Yantsche and cousins Ida and Moses like a warm blanket.

I know that playing Jewish wedding dances on a clarinet at a concentration camp might be viewed as crazy. I was okay with being temporarily crazy. Acting crazy in a crazy place is okay. It's better than okay. It's the way to be. How else should one act? But I wouldn't want to offend anyone, or get into their quiet space after they had come from who knows where to be at the final resting place of their lost families.

I found Belzec's website. It shouted rules. Open flames, like matches and candles, were not permitted— so much for lighting memorial candles. No loud noises. I didn't consider my clarinet playing as noise, but I was swayed.

Then I read a story in the *Atlanta Constitution* describing a Holocaust survivor who had created a commotion when he did a dance at Auschwitz to celebrate his survival. The article went on to explain that he was caught on film, which was used by Holocaust deniers somehow to their advantage.

So much for my clarinet.

I returned a questionnaire on the website to the Belzec museum. They wanted to make the names of victims public, not keep them anonymous as hitler had wanted. I sent them a picture of Malka strolling on a busy street in Marienbad, 1935.

I was going to see more synagogues without insides, without kishkes; more exhibits in hitler's museum to the lost race. I thought when I returned from this trip that I would visit every synagogue in Atlanta, each on a different Sabbath, and appreciate Jewish life in this Golden Age of World Jewry.

Just a week before I left, I read a story on the internet of the trial of a former Belzec guard. It was supposed to be the last big nazi war crimes trial in Germany. The article included a picture of Samuel Kunz and his buddies in front of a house in the concentration camp in 1940. He was indicted on charges of taking victims from trains, leading them into gas chambers, and throwing corpses into mass graves. I felt as if that story was written to fortify me.

Kunz died before coming to trial. "I was only carrying out orders," he had said.

I chose a letter from my grandmother to take with me to Poland for David to translate. Then I noticed it came from another address in Gorlice, not Piekarska 2, but from a place called Krotka 1. Two days before I left for Poland, I stayed up till two a.m. on the internet, trying to find Krotka 1. I found a map of Gorlice, circa 1942, hand-drawn by a resident. I wondered where the map had spent its days between the war and finding this cozy spot in the digital world. I was able to match it roughly with the Google street maps, except for the thick dashed lines drawn in the area of Piekarska. The key on the hand-drawn map beside the dashes said "granica."

When I found that granica meant "boundary" in Polish, a shiver ran through me. It was the boundary created between the Jewish and Christian populations of Gorlice. The nazis had walled in the Jewish neighborhood of Gorlice, and my grandmother was imprisoned inside the walls, in the ghetto. That night I looked at all her letters. The earlier ones were from Piekarska, the later ones from Krotka.

I reread all of my grandmother's letters and I couldn't find anywhere where she said that she had been moved, or that there was a ghetto in Gorlice. If she had written about a ghetto, or a move, the letter had been intercepted by the nazi censors to keep up their charade.

I don't know why I thought about a story that a cousin had told me. Malka had some illness while she lived in Germany, and the doctor said that the cure was for her to eat ham. Yes, it sounded like a silly story about my kosher grandmother. So, she got a special pan that she kept separate from her other kosher pans and cooked her ham in it. I wondered if the store at Piekarska 2 sold pans. If so, I might get a pan for my breakfast friend.

However, upon closer examination of the internet site, it seemed that Piekarska 2 was now an appliance store. I wondered if I should call my friend and ask if he needed a washing machine?

Chapter 25

The Room with the Betampte Kitchen
(The Room with the Cozy Kitchen)

I packed up all my intrigues and imaginings and drove them to the airport. The security line moved quickly. Boarding was uneventful. But when I fastened my seatbelt something clicked, and for the first time I felt I had quelled weeks, months, and maybe years of assorted anxieties over traveling to Poland. Just as the calm had settled in; however, the pilot announced a mechanical problem, something about the tail section of the plane. I didn't like the potential delay, but was happier to have heard the news on the ground, rather than at 35,000 feet up in the sky.

The passengers were asked to exit the plane, and after a few hours in the airport lounge, I wanted to let David know I'd be late for our planned rendezvous the next day in Warsaw. He was the only person I knew who still didn't carry a cellphone, so I called the hotel desk in Warsaw to leave a message. At one dollar a minute for a phone call to Poland, I quickly explained the situation to the English-speaking operator and left a 1940s telegramish line.

"Tell him Peter's plane is three hours late."

I arrived in Paris at eleven a.m., but my body clock read four p.m., New York time. I had missed my connecting flight, and it took me a few moments to get acclimated before I could join the queue to rebook to Warsaw. A little boy on the line held a stuffed ragdoll under his arm. He rubbed his eyes with tight little fists, while machinegun-carrying soldiers patrolled the terminal. We planned to be in Belzec in a few days. I still wasn't ready.

I arrived at the hotel in Warsaw late in the afternoon, and I was pleasantly surprised to see David reading a book in the lobby.

"Did you get my message?" I asked.

"No, but I figured out what was going on. Check in, and they'll give you a ticket for a free beer," he said. We sat in the lobby for hours and caught up.

The following morning, we picked up the rental car near the hotel. I filled out paperwork with the clerk, while David browsed a display of tourist brochures. He didn't have an international driver's license, so I was the driver. He'd navigate. I asked the fellow behind the counter, "What do I do if I get a flat tire?"

He pointed to the rental agreement. "Call this num-

ber. We'll send someone, but maybe not late at night."
He smiled. I didn't.

The air conditioning in the tiny rental office made
us so cold, we were glad to get outside. We stowed our bags
in the car. I changed 100 dollars for 299 zloty at the
exchange across the road, and we got underway. I handed
David the driving directions I had printed at home from
the internet. He was already holding his own map.

We approached Gorlice from the east, after having
passed through Rzezov, Jaslo, and Biecz. We were on the
road for a few days after visiting Pulawy, the home of
David's ancestors, driving out of the foothills of the
Carpathian Mountains to panoramic views of farm
country at harvest time. Farmers burned debris, and
while the air smelled of smoke, a haze framed the scene,
almost picture-postcard perfect.

"Lots of Jews used to live here," I said to David.

"Lots of Jews," he echoed.

"Now there are none."

I thought of how many Jewish people, frightened for
their lives, may have been hidden on these farms during the war – in these buildings and in these piles of
hay, over here, and some over there. People died on this
road.

Thirty minutes later, we stopped in a village, in a
little restaurant. The waitress, who didn't speak much
English, handed us menus. We said, "Perogies." Then I
used my favorite phrase, the only Polish sentence I
knew.

"Ne moovyeh dobjeh po polskoo."

The waitress launched into more Polish. I was puzzled. I had just told her that I didn't speak Polish.

"No, your Polish is very good," she said to me in English.

The waitress took the menus and walked away. David burst out laughing.

"You should have seen your face when she started speaking Polish to you. It's happened before on our trip when you used that phrase. How do you say it?

"Ne moovyeh dobjeh po polskoo."

He repeated, "Ne moov ...what was that again?"

I spoke the phrase more slowly.

"In the past few days you've said it so many times that by now it sounds like you can speak the language," David said.

I pulled out my phrase book and double-checked what I was saying. My favorite Polish sentence actually meant, "My Polish is not so good," rather than what I needed to say, which was "I don't speak Polish. Not one word."

My tongue was getting accustomed to this Polish place, having been bathed during the last few days in kasha, herring, onions, borscht and perogies. My tongue was learning some of the sounds of this surprising language, whose words looked like the tiles that remained on the rack at the end of the Scrabble game.

We headed out after lunch; next stop Gorlice. I was eager to get there and at the same time fearful. I had thought about going to my grandmother's place for so long. How would the real thing compare to my imagination?

It was early in the afternoon, and we were driving slowly on the winding road. David was looking in his guidebook.

"One of the oldest wooden churches in Poland is nearby. I'd like to go see it."

I was ready for Gorlice. I had been thinking about being there for years, and now I just wanted to push ahead, but David seemed to really want to see that church.

"Are you sure you want to go? There's nothing else around here."

"Yes, I see it on the map. It's practically on the way. Let's go. It won't take long."

David wanted to see the five-hundred-year-old church at Binarowa and drive through Biecz, one of the oldest towns in Poland. At that moment, I didn't care. I was mere miles from my grandmother's apartment, and all I wanted to do was get to Gorlice. I was working on an unfinished dream. But I gave in.

We turned off the two-lane onto a smaller winding road and followed the signs to the old church. A tour bus was driving out as we pulled in. We went inside the church, but I felt like a stranger, as if I shouldn't be there. David signed the guestbook. I didn't. The guide, or caretaker, a young woman, pointed to the book and said something to me in Polish. I shook my head. I wondered if they wanted to send me notices of future church events. She pointed to different places on the floor where the tiles were broken and were in various states of repair. She must have told us in Polish to watch where we walked.

A man and a woman appeared from another room. He was wearing a "Chicago" T-shirt, and carried a camera slung around his neck. He appeared inquisitive about the sympathetic vibrations he felt in this place, the silent hum of *his* origin. Through the thick lenses of his glasses he was looking for evidence of his DNA in the old place. But something was pushing me out of the church.

"I'll wait outside for you," I said to David.

I didn't think about it until later, but I had something in common with the fellow in the Chicago T-shirt. We had roots in similar ground, but on opposite sides of the fence. And we were both helpless to resist such a strange wind that had blown us to that place.

As we drove closer to Gorlice, I got the willies. The skin down my back felt like it had when I went to school without my homework or came into class late. It was the sweaty dream of being in Chinese 401 for the first time as the final exam blue-books were handed out. My stomach felt like it had after taking the dare and becoming that ten-year-old boy, alone, under the basement stairs in the dark.

Our arrival in Gorlice happened too quickly, even though an occasional tractor or bicycle rider slowed the flow of traffic on our two-lane winding road. It wasn't that the car was speeding or that the farms were flying by. It was a thought that I had had years ago. And it was coming up the road behind me. It had been following from a distance and now was closing in.

It had nudged me to dance to the klezmer music in my parents' kitchen. It had brought the prisoners to the synagogue when I played my clarinet. It had sent me my grandmother's letters. I couldn't see this hundred-ton locomotive bearing down on me in the rearview mirror, even though it was inches from the rear bumper and loomed over the back window. But I could feel it pushing me forward. I couldn't get out of its way. I couldn't get off the tracks.

I had always been on this train.

Then suddenly I saw it flash in front of me, the painted green metal road sign that said "Gorlice, 10 Km." It was neon. It was Hollywood.

If I had been alone, I would have pulled over and sat on the side of the road and scratched my head, pondering what to do next. I wasn't ready to continue. I didn't know what I had to do to get comfortable with the idea of walking on the same streets that my family had walked for generations, most recently my grandmother and her brothers. More intriguing however, was finding the place where the letters in the suitcase had come from.

The room with the betampte kitchen.

Had I been alone, I might have stalled. I might have turned back and gone the next day. But I didn't suggest to David that we wait a day to continue. I didn't say anything. I just kept my foot on the gas.

We drove into the town of Gorlice but couldn't find Piekarska, my grandmother's street. We drove around for a bit and found Gorlice had an older city at the top of a hill and a newer city down below. It is not so easy to get a map of Gorlice, Poland, when you live in Atlanta, Georgia. The best I could do was to print a few pages of a Google map, zoomed in close enough so I could read some street names. But those diagrams proved more difficult to read than I had imagined. I had thought that *now* should look like *then*.

After driving in circles for a while, I recognized a few of the street names from my research. I parked the car at the end of Strozowska, a street that ran into the rynek. I wanted to be as close to the market square as possible but had to park a few streets away because even in downtown Gorlice, there were no available parking spaces. I parked European-style, front-end first, two wheels on the sidewalk. Driving up over the curb felt like something I'd do when abandoning a broken-down car. Two girls sitting on the wall watched. We got out of the car, and an old man walking by stopped and stared as I pulled the Google map from my knapsack.

We walked down the street, past Krakowska and Strazacka, but no Piekarska. We passed a florist's shop, and I stopped to look in the window. Bunches of yellow flowers looked up at me from their water-filled buckets. I thought of getting a bunch for my grandmother, but it would have been too awkward to have to explain who the flowers were for, so I kept walking, with one foot in *then* and one foot in *now*.

We continued down the street, and then there it was: the number two, a large white number on a blue background above the left corner of a doorway. It popped up right in front of me like in a cartoon movie. Above the number was Ul. Piekarska. Ul. is the Polish abbreviation for "street." The tan façade of the building looked modern, especially the parts covered with signs advertising the commercial establishments in the building.

I turned to David and pointed.

"That's it. There it is."

This was my grandmother's house. David, who was leaning on a wall across the street, was smiling but not nearly as impressed as I, and certainly not as impressed as my ten-year-old's imagination at being in front of his grandmother's house. Pedestrians on the narrow sidewalk were also not so impressed with Piekarska 2 and appeared eager for me to get out of their way. But my ten-year-old's imagination was jumping up and down inside my skin.

"This is it! This is where my grandmother's letters came from," I said out loud to no one in particular.

Did I think that would mean anything to the passersby? I wanted to tell them the whole story, but that would have been impossible. This was Poland 2010, not 1940. I spoke English, they spoke Polish. And no one really cared. Besides, I was still undercover. I still wanted to be invisible in Poland, though the summer heat had forced me to shed my outer skin of a jacket.

At that moment, I knew how Neil Armstrong must have felt when he walked on the moon. I knew how Jacques Cousteau must have felt when he unearthed a sunken treasure of golden doubloons buried for hundreds of years under the sea. Although the people on the sidewalk walked right past, this treasure was not hidden, not from *my* eyes.

Some pedestrians stared at me when I took pictures. A group of women smiled as I posed for a picture that David snapped from across the narrow street—a photo of me standing in front of my grandmother's house. Those women knew that for a moment, I was Neil Armstrong.

I walked slowly up the two steps from the sidewalk through the open double door into Piekarska 2. I didn't want to miss anything. It was an older-style wooden door with a three-paneled transom. I was in my grandmother's place and thought I was dreaming. I peered down a dark hallway at a narrow flight of stairs with barely enough room on a step for two people to stand together.

As I stepped into the vestibule it seemed as if things were rushing at me faster than I could absorb them, but it was only my eyes adjusting to the change in light. The hall was backlit by a small window on the landing. I was afraid I would miss some important facet, so I stood still until I could focus and absorb all the details. The hallway and the stairs looked older than the building façade, which had undergone a facelift. The walls on either side of the staircase were painted an unimaginative green, the bottom half darker than the lime color above. The stairs looked like an original artery.

I ascended the thirteen steps to the next landing, not the smooth spiral corkscrew leading to a light-house tower, but a straight path that stopped to rest before continuing higher to the next stage. Maybe that's how time flowed, the past and the present connecting, meeting on the landing where I stood.

Some of the gray stone steps were chipped at their front edges and all had been worn smooth by years of soles and heels. It looked as though the freshly painted, black iron handrail had been added as an afterthought. I imagined my grandmother had trudged up and down these stairs a thousand times, to and from the synagogue, going to the rynek, coming from the rynek. I could see her carrying a few potatoes or some kasha for stuffed cabbage—glompki in Polish, הַאֶלְעבצעס, halubtshus in Yiddish. Maybe she bought some beets in the market for borscht or flour for Shabbat challah.

My grandmother stopped on the landing for a moment and caught her breath before continuing up to her room with the betampte kitchen. She opened her door and put down her goods, wrapped in a newspaper, on a small table.

I, too, stopped on the landing, which led to four or five more steps up to the second floor, where someone's black bicycle leaned against the wall.

She is standing in the doorway, a little grayer than I had imagined, a little thinner. Her hair is textured like long strands of Brillo pulled back tightly behind her head. She is wearing a blue apron that is missing its front pockets. In their place, like a pair of eyes, are two blue islands, surrounded by the faded fabric. The former pockets patch the fraying bottom of the apron on which she is drying her hands.

I'm nervous and excited. I want to know about her, about her parents, where they came from, but mostly about my father. I don't know what to say, where to begin. I've forgotten why I've come and where I am.

We stare at each other for a moment, not saying a word, sizing each other up, our eyes scanning, head to toe and back up again, gazing into each other's faces. There is a beam between us. Her eyes are hazel like my father's. She eyes me so intensely I have to look away. She is peering inside of me. She extends her hands, reaches up and takes my face in them. Her hands are soft, wrinkled and fragrant—soap and roses. She wears no jewelry. Her eyes are closed almost as if she is praying or transmitting something to me. She opens her arms for a hug and I oblige. She is breathing very deeply, and I feel her chest heaving against mine. I don't know how long to stand like that. I take a step back, and we are almost face to face. She studies me, smiles, and says in a very heavy German accent, "You look like Max," and I say, "So do you."

Then I think, what a silly thing I've just said.

She closes her eyes for a second. Her head bobs two or three times, a gesture that I have seen in my Aunt Sidy, Malka's daughter. She turns in the doorway, putting one arm around my shoulder, and with her hand outstretched, shows me the way into her apartment.

My grandmother guides me into the room with the *betampte* kitchen. The smell of just-baked bread mixes in the air with the strong sunlight coming through the windows.

I wish that I had bought the cut flowers for her when we passed the florist shop in the square. I feel guilty coming empty-handed.

My grandmother motions to a chair at the round table. "Sit, please," she says.

Each of the four chairs looks different from the next. I pick the closest.

"You must have had a long trip. Are you tired, *shafaleh?*" she asks.

My aunt Sidy used to call me *shafaleh*, the diminutive of *shafe*—sheep in German.

I say, "I don't know. I'm so excited to see you, I can't feel anything."

"How did you know where I was?

"I read your letters...was that all right?"

"Ach, Max saves everything."

She sighs and waves a hand. She takes a picture from a drawer. It is of my father. The same picture is in his suitcase. She holds it in her hand and regards it sadly as she speaks.

"I didn't know what happened to him after the mail stopped. I knew how worried he was," she says.

"He never talked about you, or about what happened."

"My heart broke when I read his letters. He felt so guilty about leaving me here when he went to Amerika, but I forgave him long ago. I just wanted him to live and to be happy."

"Grandmother, I came to visit you in Leipzig."

"Yes, I know."

"I played a song for you on my clarinet. Did you hear it?"

She smiles. "You played the Heyser Bulgar. I danced to it at my wedding. How did you know?"

I had a lump in my throat and my eyes were tearing.

"Max tried to save you, but your papers didn't come in time."

"Tell me about your mother. Was she good to Max?"

"She was the best."

"Do you have her picture?"

I shook my head.

"I wanted him to marry Lola," my grandmother said.

We were rushing. Both of us knew that our time together was closing.

"What did you miss, grandmother? What did you want if you could have had anything?"

She thought for a moment.

"I wished that G-d would have saved the Jews of the world."

"He did. You have eight grandchildren. I'm the youngest."

She begins to cry.

The outside door leading to the street at the bottom of the stairs slams with a bang. My grandmother's door swings open, and I feel something blow by me and touch me on the cheek. The wind must have blown through the doors.

I looked over the rail toward the downstairs door, and when I looked back I was facing the open doorway leading into my grandmother's apartment. I stood on the landing and peered through her open door, but despite having traveled so far to come here I felt awkward going inside. I entered into a small room, bright, freshly painted white, with a new wooden floor. It was an empty room, a poster of a woman on the wall.

Through the next doorway on the left were a few chairs. Three or four teenaged girls were chatting on their cellphones. I don't think they noticed me. Inside the next doorway a woman sat in a chair, her hair, streaked with red, combed out in a witchlike do. She sat with a towel around her neck. Pieces of foil stuck in her hair. Our eyes met, and I thought when she looked away, down toward the floor, *she* wanted to be invisible. I knew what that was like, because I wanted to be invisible in Poland. But what she was doing in my grandmother's kitchen?

My grandmother's apartment with the betampte kitchen had become a hair salon.

Reality trumps imagination.

I retreated into the waiting area. The door behind me opened, and a scruffy-looking guy looked me up and down. We were both going to say, "What are you doing here?" but he pushed past me and went down the stairs.

I thought about getting my hair cut in my grandmother's kitchen. I could have made the motion of snipping scissors to the woman cutting hair, pointed to my head, and sat down in a chair. But I didn't know how to say, "the usual," or "a little off over the ears." I kept my hair.

I had landed in my grandmother's kitchen and wanted to sit at the table where she had sat when she wrote those letters to my father, the letters that lived in the suitcase. I wanted to have a cup of coffee with her while she wrote. I was ready to see her worn armchair, a lace doily on a wooden table, her Sabbath candlesticks. Perhaps my great-uncle, Yantsche, would be sitting at the table as he had done before when my grandmother wrote her letters. I could see his face with its greying beard, his head covered with a rumpled cap, his work apron from the shoe maker's shop down the street.

But my imagination had been defeated. There was not one shred of evidence, not one reminder that my grandmother had ever lived at Piekarska 2, in the room with the betampte kitchen.

After all those years I had come back to an empty house, stripped of my grandmother's spirit. Part of me, the ten-year-old inside, was looking for more—a celebration, an acknowledgement, a reward. He was wounded and thought it might have been better if we had never come at all. Then he could have imagined forever. But part of me knew to move on. I wasn't going to have that last dance with my grandmother, she was gone from here; but we had shared this same place, and I was glad for that.

I had chased a spirit and gotten so close, its fluttering wings had brushed my face.

♦

Not knowing what else to do, I could have lingered. But why? What now?

I was numb.

David was standing on the stairs when I came out of the hairdresser's place. It wasn't the room with the betampte kitchen anymore. Seventy years passed in the time it took to walk down a flight of stairs.

"Come on, let's go," I said. "I did it. I saw it."

I was exhausted and, in a way, defeated. We walked quietly down the steps to the street. The way out looked so different. I thought I had just been there. I paused on the landing where the past met the present. It flowed through me, that breeze in the hallway, and nudged me down the stairs between the lime green walls.

At the front door the light of the summer sun made me squint, and a current flowing down the street carried us away from the house. I turned back to look once or twice at the hairdresser's place.

♦

A little way down the street on the other side of the road, at number 3 Piekarska, was a long, two-story building with light gray, almost white stucco walls. Maybe it was the familiar shape of the windows that said "synagogue" to me. They resembled the windows in a synagogue I had attended as a boy in Brooklyn. A plaque high up on a wall, etched in Polish, said something about hitler and the Jews.

But the nearest doorway was dark, and the rusted knob and splintered frame didn't match the look of the up-to-date façade. A collection of spiderwebs told me this door hadn't been opened in a while, but it was the doorway I needed to go through. It had swung open years ago for my grandmother and my uncles, Yantsche and Selig. I tried the knob, thinking it would admit me, but the past was nailed shut.

We walked down the sidewalk, and at the end of the street was an open door. I stuck my head in the doorway of what I thought would be a synagogue. But I ended up in a bakery. A gaggle of gears ground in my head. A voice called from way down a dark hallway. My grandmother lived on Piekarska. Piekar is an oven, piekarz a baker, in Polish. My shtetl book told of my great grandmother who managed the family bakery, and my grandfather, the cantor in the synagogue, who gave honey cake from the bakery to the children on holidays.

Perhaps I was standing in the doorway of my great-grandmother's shop. I couldn't help but think of my grandmother writing to my father in 1939 from her betampte kitchen across the street, bemoaning the nazi-instigated takeover of the family bakery and the closing of the synagogue. The censor would have thrown *that* letter into the fire, with a laugh. The smell of fresh bread, kneaded by strange hands, creeping into my grandmother's apartment early every morning must have tormented her.

This was the bakery I had read about, the former 1939 synagogue. My imagination had been pulled here years earlier, after I opened the suitcase and read the invitation to my cousin's 1939 Gorlice wedding. This was the synagogue with the painting of the two lions holding the tablets of the Ten Commandments high up on the ceiling. I had to see that ceiling. I knew my grandmother and her brothers had.

We went around the corner to find an entrance to the sanctuary, but there were no other doorways. We went back to the bakery, and as I entered, I faced two white doors with green lettering across their tops. But I didn't understand the Polish words. I had come so far to face the memories in this place where my ancestors had come to talk to G-d, and they were just behind that door with the green writing.

David and I stood in the customer area of the bakery, so small there would not have been room for a third person, except of course if my grandmother or my great-uncle Yantsche had walked in. To my right, a cash register sat on a cluttered counter. It separated the customer space from the baked goods. I don't know how long we stood there before a young woman popped up from behind the counter. The thought bubble over her head said: He's not a regular customer, and tourists didn't come around here much, so just exactly what does he want?

But she said in Polish, "Projyeh." Please.

She wanted me to order. *I* wanted to see the inside of the old synagogue. Maybe she saw the thought bubble over my head. And even though the look on someone's face or the tilt of a head doesn't always need a translation, I knew I was going to have to come up with the right words to get inside—though I thought any stranger who came into this store on Piekarska in Gorlice, Poland would be looking for his roots, not for bread.

I looked over the counter at the freshly baked breads. The loaves on the downward-slanting shelves were long and rectangular, others dark, round, or oblong. On the floor behind the counter were round straw baskets filled with large crusty breads. The aroma made my mouth water. I pointed to some cookies on the shelf behind the counter.

I was stalling. I needed an excuse to spend more time in this place where my ancestors had walked, and to think of how to strike up a conversation with a total stranger, in a language I couldn't speak. The cashier saw me point and reached for a loaf of bread. I shook my head and pointed to the left. She put her hand beside another loaf. I shook my head again and pointed down to a lower shelf. She took a large Styrofoam tray of cookies wrapped in clear plastic and put it on the counter. I mimed "smaller" and said, "mawy."

She hunted at the back of a shelf and returned with a smaller package. I nodded. Then one of the white doors with the green writing opened, and I caught a glimpse inside of what must have been the old synagogue. It was dark, and I could only see the baker in his white apron, some bread-making equipment, a cart with metal trays and a huge stainless-steel mixing bowl. Polish would have come in handy. I turned to David and pointed inside the door again.

"That's where I want to be," I said. He looked puzzled.

"That's the inside of the old synagogue. The painting of the lions is on the ceiling."

I smiled at the cashier and pointed inside the door. She stared at me. I pointed to myself, and then pointed inside the door. She still stared at me.

David and I pulled out our phrase books and thumbed through the pages. He said, "I could ask her if there are breadcrumbs on the pork chops." It was an awkward moment for a laugh, but I couldn't hold back. If I had had any chance of getting to the other side of the counter, I had just laughed it away. Then David said to the woman, "Can we go inside?"

She launched into a Polish conversation with the baker and two other women sitting behind the door. Then she shook her head and said something in Polish to us that sounded like, "Why do people ask to go inside the factory? You cannot." And then she smiled.

I could have told her my family owned a bakery in town, maybe this one, and my great-grandfather sang in this synagogue. I could have told her I was trying to get a glimpse of the footprints of my ancestors who had lived here for generations until the nazis came to town and trucked them all off to die in a concentration camp.

This synagogue, across the street from my grandmother's apartment, with its painted lions on the ceiling, was a monument in a place that had wiped clean the traces of Jewish life that once flourished. I wanted the picture of those lions for my mind's eye. But I didn't know how to say all that in Polish. I paid for my cookies, and David and I left.

It didn't strike me then, but now I look back on how crushed I was not to have found even one crumb of evidence pointing to my grandmother's existence. Then I wandered into a *bakery*. Perhaps it was my family's.

♦

I needed to sit down. What had just happened?

We found a nearby pub, which was empty at three o'clock in the afternoon. I went to the bar, ordered two beers, and watched every drop pour from the painfully slow tap into the two mugs. David and I sat at a table near the window.

"I don't know where to begin. I'm numb. It was all so bizarre," I said. "I wouldn't be surprised if it took me years to make some logic of all this."

"When did you realize it was a hair salon?' David asked.

"Not until I saw the woman with the tin foil in her hair."

"And what about that guy? What was he doing there?"

"Yeah. I wanted to ask him why he was in my grandmother's kitchen."

"Sorry I made you laugh in the bakery. You looked so serious."

"I really wanted to get inside that door, but I didn't know how. It was so frustrating. I felt like I was gagged. Then your question about the breadcrumbs on the pork chops was so crazy, it struck my funny bone.

David laughed.

"I guess it wasn't meant to be. Maybe I'm expecting too much of this trip," I said.

♦

It was a very hot day, and the first long sip of beer was refreshing. I took the cookies from my knapsack, put them on the table, and we started eating. They tasted so familiar that they brought me back to Brooklyn, to my corner, the Garden Bakery on Avenue P and East 4ᵗʰ Street.

I have a sweet tooth with a memory. It recognized the taste of the light-colored cookie flour, a little crumbly, almost sandy. It was the foundation for many Garden Bakery cookies I had eaten as a boy, sometimes after Saturday services at synagogue, sometimes after dinner at my mother's kitchen table. They came out of a white cardboard box tied with a thin red-striped string that we used to play cat's cradle with after dessert. I recognized from my childhood the flower-petal-shaped cookie with the red jam in the center and the cookies in two kinds of clam shell shapes with a line of chocolate in between the shells.

I wanted to text my brother in Madison saying, "I'm here in Gorlice, eating cookies from the Garden Bakery," when David said, "These remind me of a Jewish bakery near where I lived in Detroit when I was a kid." He was trying to open the package from the other end to get at his favorite finger-long cookie covered in strawberry jam.

It was odd how a place so strange and uncomfortable could be made so familiar by a cookie and how time could be compressed into the shape of a bit of baked dough, flavored by the past. And it was odd how this experience was fed to me in the bakery across the street from my grandmother's house, perhaps even the family bakery one hundred years ago. It was a taste I had known my whole life.

We needed a change of scenery and didn't get to translate a letter in the pub. We went down the street to the rynek and took a table in a café.

"Feel like reading a letter?" I asked David.

"Sure," he said.

We sat so close to my grandmother's place I could have seen her in the window as David translated a letter to my father.

It was dated November 17, 1941. On that same day, my research told me, eight Jews were executed for going outside the Warsaw ghetto without permission. Six were women. And on that day, a Luftwaffe General Udet apparently shot himself dead in a Berlin hotel. There were rumors he was ordered to commit suicide.

I slid the frail sheet of paper out of its envelope and handed it across the table.

David began: "November 17, 1941 - Gorlice My Dear Good Max:

> I haven't received any mail from you in a while, nor have I received any mail from dear Lola in the last two weeks. I don't know what to think, and from Nunka I know nothing, and the poor children are now all alone because their father has died. They are without supplies and all alone in a strange place. I have no peace because of the children. Selig died during the operation – an intestinal twisting. I wouldn't have written to you about it except that I want you to tell Heinrich. Otherwise we give you my dear Max only the best... It's good only to hear good things from you. And also from Bertha I haven't received mail. When you write Sidy please give her and her husband my greeting. This is all not much joy. I wrote Lola on her birthday and she hasn't answered. Otherwise nothing is new. I greet you and kiss you warmly. Greet all the relatives for me. Please write Uncle. Send him my greetings. Here all the relatives send you greetings.

> From your mother who loves you and wishes you the best.

And there I was, with a letter from my grandmother she had written to my father seventy years ago from this place. I wondered if some cosmic counter clicked off the completed cycle. I felt as if time had been removed. This letter was addressed from Krotka 1, inside the ghetto.

It was the last letter.

David and I sat in the rynek, finished our coffee, and I slid the letter back into a book in my knapsack for safekeeping.

"So, my uncle Selig died on the operating table," I said. "At least the nazis didn't get him."

"Who's Heinrich?" David asked.

"My great-uncle, Malka's youngest brother. He's sometimes Henry, Heinrich, or Chaskal. But everyone called him Oncle. I remember him. He came to our house in Brooklyn once. I must have been about ten."

"Was he the only survivor in your family of his generation?"

"I think so."

♦

I motioned across the square. "Let's look at that tourist map over there. Maybe we can find the Jewish cemetery."

We examined a map of the city that stood six feet high, mounted in a Plexiglas frame. We compared the map to the descriptions of the cemetery location in our guidebooks. We were both stumped. Then a name jumped off the map at me.

"Krotka," I said.

I pointed to the name on the map.

"That's where the letter came from, Krotka 1."

"Come on, I'll show you," David said, and was off like a homing pigeon, heading out of the square. With one arm waving over his shoulder, he motioned for me to follow him up a small street. We passed a nameless road, then another.

"This must be it," he said.

I walked up the street, trying to find an address with a street name. In the middle of the block I turned onto a road with one house beside a parking lot. The address of the house was Krotka 1. It was the house inside the ghetto walls from which the last letters had come. My grandmother never mentioned that she had been forced to move out of the room with the betampte kitchen and was living in the ghetto. The censor must have gotten that letter.

A scaffold supported the façade of Krotka 1, its old face bearing the weight of memories. Red flowers grew in a box on a first-floor windowsill. A ghetto and red flowers didn't fit together in my picture.

People were living in Krotka 1's apartments. Inside the front door, hanging on the wall in a frame, was a black-and-white picture of a man above a typed page of Polish text. I heard the clack-clack-clack of old typewriter keys in my mind. The man inside the picture frame had lived in this house, in Krotka 1, a partisan during the war. I would have liked to have known what the short story said. Did he help the ghetto dwellers? Did he know my grandmother?

A shiny plaque on the front of the building said something in Polish about hitler in 1939. The side of the house, next to a parking lot, was a sad, blank gray wall, with no windows except for one, like an eye at the top. Krotka 1 had stood shoulder to shoulder with another house when it was built. There was no use for windows on the side, but the other house had been knocked down, or fell down, and that window added more recently.

I studied the thick, dashed lines on the hand-drawn map I had found on the internet, the map made by a Gorlice resident during the war. I held the map out toward the street and tried to find the outline of the granica, the ghetto walls, near the sidewalk. I kicked in the dirt at the edge of the sidewalk looking for traces of the old walls, and saw the blemish bordering the cobblestones running down the street. That scar hadn't healed in all these years.

I thought about my grandmother, cooped up in an apartment just over there with who-knows-how-many strangers during a cold Polish winter, with not enough to eat - right there, in the apartment with the flower box and the red flowers.

I texted my brother. "I'm standing in front of the ghetto apartment where our grandmother lived." It was a very lonely place.

"I'm with you," came his distant hug.

It was about five o'clock on Friday afternoon in the old Jewish neighborhood of Gorlice. Sabbath approached, and although there were no Jews in Gorlice any longer, I could feel the spirits of the Jewish population rushing to get ready for the Day of Rest. Challah baked in the ovens as men hurried home to get ready for Mincha, the afternoon service. My grandmother was by herself, but when I went past her place I found the door leading up to her apartment closed tightly.

I was happy to leave Gorlice behind, and also sad to leave Gorlice thinking how my grandmother, her brothers, and their families had all been murdered for being Jewish. And I was anxious, because I felt like I was leaving something behind, something I should have taken care of. There was something else, but I didn't know what it could be. I felt it behind me, in a place I couldn't see.

Nevertheless, I was leaving with the intent of never returning to this place.

Chapter 26

Where is the Sabbath?

We left Gorlice late Friday afternoon and arrived in Nowy Sacz under darkening clouds. David's perfect map-reading ability had disappeared, so we circled and circled through the city in the pouring rain looking for a hotel. Beneath flickering lightning, the Hotel Panorama at the end of a narrow road appeared to offer a sweeping view overlooking the Dunajec River. I sat behind the wheel of our rented car, parked on the cobblestone street, while David went inside to inquire about a room.

After visiting Gorlice, I was drained. I felt like I was part of the upholstery's pattern on the driver's seat. An image appeared in the mirror outside my door: black rain clouds reflected in the mirror behind me with a bright sky in front, but I was too tired to dig my camera out of the trunk. The photo could have been the metaphor for the trip.

David returned in a few minutes. "The hotel is all booked. Let's try somewhere else."

We tried to find the Hotel Beskid, advertised in our tour guides. After a few more circles around town in the pouring rain, we found it on a side street we had driven past at least three times before. Looking down onto the street a few minutes later from our sixth-floor window, I noticed the rain had stopped, and I needed to stretch my legs. I had been driving for longer than I wanted to be cooped up in a car. I needed to process Gorlice. But there was a voicemail on my phone from my wife, who was with the kids in North Carolina.

"American Express called," she said. "They have recorded a suspicious charge to your card made from Turkey, and they want to cancel it."

"Can you believe that?" I said to David. "American Express wants to cancel my card."

He shook his head.

"And I'm such a good customer."

"You'd better call them."

"Wanna take a walk?"

"No, I'm just going to relax up here," David said, returning to his book.

I took the elevator down and went through the lobby and out the front the door into the cool air, scrubbed clean by the hard rain. The air was so clear it seemed I could look down the wide Boleslawa Limanowskiego and see forever, maybe into the past.

I called my wife, and my oldest son answered her phone. She was driving, so he acted as the go-between in our conversation. After we resolved the credit card issue I asked him to pass the phone to the back seat, and I spoke to my other children. I wished they all could have been here with me to glimpse *their* past.

That evening I felt like a drink, so I asked in the lobby if there was a liquor store nearby. I was directed a few hundred meters down the street. It was late, maybe about midnight. No one was on the street, and only an occasional car passed. The stores were closed. I saw some brighter lights a few streets down, and I kept walking in that direction until I came to, what in Atlanta would be called, a strip mall. There was one open store, a combination twenty-four-hour grocery, drugstore, and liquor store. I wanted a little Zubrovka, the vodka with the buffalo on the label and a blade of bison grass inside. I entered the store and spied a small bottle of the stuff on a front shelf. I pointed.

"Zubrovka," I said, like a native, to the woman behind the counter. I paid her the equivalent of a couple of dollars in Zlotys, the small bottle only slightly more expensive than water. I stuffed it into a pocket of my jacket. Ten minutes later David and I sat in our hotel room, enjoying the mellow drink and talking about the day.

"How long do you think it will take us to get far enough away from this place to get some perspective on what we've seen?" I asked.

David shrugged and shook his head. "Such a good question. I think quite a while."

The next morning, we went to the old Dwana synagogue. Malka had written to my father in 1939 that she had celebrated Passover at her brother Mechuel's house in Nowy Sacz, so I was confident that my grandmother and my great-uncle and his family had been here in the synagogue. The big brownstone building standing on the corner didn't appear to have suffered damage in the war, and I wondered why it hadn't been burned to the ground like so many others.

Inside the skeleton of the former synagogue, the building was now part art gallery, part museum. The new tenants kept the faint heartbeat going. Pictures hung in the sanctuary, and just inside the entrance was a small museum with photos of prewar life in Nowy Sacz, as well as some religious artifacts. They were all *proof* that Jews once lived here. There was a picture of a decree that had allowed the Jews of Nowy Sacz to build a synagogue hundreds of years earlier. I examined every picture in the community-member display, hoping to find my grandmother's face or another's displaying familial attributes. I found neither.

David didn't linger inside as long as I did, so on this Sabbath morning I was alone in the empty gallery of the synagogue where my grandmother and her brother had prayed. As I stood in the middle of the floor where I thought the bimah, the altar, once stood, I faced the direction of the ark, where the scrolls of the Torah had rested more than seventy years ago. I hummed some

Sabbath songs. I sang "Aneem Zemeros," traditionally sung at the end of the Sabbath service. As I sang louder, I heard something creak upstairs in the wooden balcony, like a person adjusting herself in a chair in which she had been sitting for too long.

I ran up the stairs of the old synagogue into the balcony, the women's section. But there were no familiar faces, no surprised glances, no feathered hats or perfumed scents. There were no people or prayers. I was in an art gallery. The pictures on the walls were a modern armor, protecting the old home of community and prayer from abandonment and demolition. If there were any Jews remaining in Nowy Sacz, they too could have been exhibits in this museum. And I thought, even though it was Saturday, could there still be Shabbos in Nowy Sacz without any Jews?

I carried my thought into the park across the street from the synagogue and watched two Polish women who worked in the gallery come out of the building, lock the front door, and leave for the afternoon. They had stayed for me after closing time, and I was grateful. Maybe they had heard the singing and the wooden balcony creaking and didn't want to interrupt the visitors.

Under the blue sky, I sat on a bench in the park and thought about Shabbos. I looked at the old synagogue. I wondered: Where did Shabbos go after she saw the last Jew dragged from the ghetto?

She cried, I am sure.

Friday at sunset, she flew in a panic above cobblestone streets and peered in dread through closed windows. She did not see the white tablecloths or the Shabbos candlesticks. She did not see the braided challah, or polished-silver Kiddush cups filled with red wine. The children and mothers and fathers who had returned home from synagogue on Friday nights for the last five hundred years were gone. Shabbos had been a guest in Nowy Sacz for half the millennium, but when she saw the empty synagogue after the last Jew was gone from its ghetto, Shabbos was homeless.

Shabbos in Nowy Sacz had flown away. She had nowhere to stay, to put her hat, to rest her feet, to bless the challah, to sing songs and light the candles. Shabbos had left Nowy Sacz. Or maybe she was hiding, waiting to return to the Dwana synagogue on Friday evening to hear "Lecha Dodi," a welcome from the congregation, who would turn to face the entrance when she arrived, each happy to see the other.

♦

A small car whizzed past and dented my quiet space before colliding with a van lumbering in the rotary. I watched the occupants pile out onto the street and wave their arms as though they were swimming in air. David came up the path in the park. We located our car and drove down the street beside the Dwana synagogue and across the bridge over the Kamienica River to find the Jewish cemetery. After a couple of wrong turns, we drove past an iron gate adorned with a metal plate in the shape of a candelabra.

I parked the car behind a few others on the street as a woman unloaded a group of children from her black sedan and herded them into a house near the cemetery. A sign told us that a descendent of a Nowy Sacz resident living in New York City had arranged for the iron fence to be built around the cemetery. Now the beer bottles would collect outside the fence instead of on the cemetery grounds. The cemetery had been ransacked, fallen into disrepair. Some of the headstones were lying in the tall grass like spilled dominoes. I was surprised that a visible Jewish graveyard was there at all. David jumped up on the low stone wall and began to climb the iron fence.

"Come on, just climb over," he said.

"No, I don't think I'm going to do that."

"Why not? What are you afraid of?"

I watched him delicately lift his leg over the arrow-shaped tops of the black fence. He winced as he caught himself on one of the metal reminders. I pictured sirens and the flashing lights of Polish police cars skidding to a halt in front of the Nowy Sacz Jewish cemetery, responding to a report of vandals climbing the fence.

A moment later David jumped to the ground inside the cemetery and hurried toward the standing stones on the far side. Then he was gone from sight. I followed the fence around the perimeter of the cemetery towards the side of the graveyard facing the main street, hoping to find a legal way to get in. When I neared the end of the path, I found David on the other side of the fence.

"See if you can find any stones with Kalb, Degen, or Frauwirt. That's my family," I said.

We talked through the fence while I traced in the

air the Hebrew characters of the first letters of their names as I thought they might appear on the stones.

"Kalb is with the letter koof, Degen is a dalid, Frauwirt is a pay," I told him.

It seemed in that moment David linked with his boyhood Hebrew school lessons and made the connections. When I peered through the fence and read the inscriptions on some of the stones that were facing in my direction, I was surprised at the burial dates, the 1960s and 1970s. There must have been something of a Jewish Community revival after the war, after that odd explosion that I thought had killed the Jews but left some synagogues and cemeteries.

I turned the corner of the cemetery and saw a sign on the front gate that said the key to the entranceway was across the street with Mr. Mueller. I didn't know how we had missed the sign, but I went to see about the key. There was a buzzer on the fence that surrounded a small, neat garden in front of a private house. "Mueller" was printed under the buzzer. I rang it.

On the second floor of the house I saw the bent figure of a man at the window. He looked my way, and I made the motion of a key opening a door. He shook his head. I pointed to the cemetery across the street. Then I waited. I don't know how long I waited. I didn't know what else to do. Then a slight, neatly dressed old man came out of the house. He wore a cap, and a blue shirt, and walked painfully slowly toward me. I pointed at the cemetery gate and again made the motion of a key opening a lock. I saw a gold crown in his mouth, on the same tooth that my father had a gold crown. The old man waggled his finger and shook his head at me.

"Shabbos," he said

He walked past me to the corner.

Mr. Mueller wasn't going to open the cemetery gate for me on the Sabbath, and no, Shabbos had not left Nowy Sacz.

Chapter 27

A Terrible Place

We drove through farm country and old villages. The road was well-paved, with two and sometimes four lanes, and rotaries that reminded me of driving on Cape Cod, but without the vacation feel.

I was driving to a terrible place.

And when I thought of where I was headed, the road began to rush downhill.

When I saw the first sign for Belzec, I felt as if I was being sucked into a hole. Faster and faster we were pulled along the road. I became distracted. *What am I doing here?* I thought of turning the car around. I knew what had happened at Belzec and still hadn't prepared enough. But how could one prepare for such a place? The car was being drawn into a twilight zone.

I was going to the place where the bones of my grandmother and her brothers and their wives and sons and daughters lay under the earth, burnt and ground into bits. During WWII, the commandant of Auschwitz, on a tour of Belzec, had said, "This is a terrible place." The nazis created a farm on the site to disguise the camp. My family lay under the farmer's fields.

I kept my foot on the gas. My stomach twisted with lightning crackling from rib to rib. My right arm and my right hand on the steering wheel began to twitch and flutter as though they belonged to another. I drove with my left hand. I felt like I had drunk five cups of coffee – not alert, but nervous and edgy.

David was talking. I didn't tell him I couldn't hear his words. We were driving beside railroad tracks, and my brain sped to keep up with the invisible train delivering prisoners, stuffed shoulder to shoulder. I saw a smoke stack in the distance and an old orange-brown brick building on the other side of the tracks. The captives had gone up in smoke. I had a lump in my throat and my eyes teared. I was near Belzec, near the place where my ten-year-old's imagination had arranged for my father to avenge the murder of my grandmother in a sniper attack. I was in the space between my imagination and reality, only it wasn't a space. It was the only place, and it was everywhere.

It came up quickly. The railroad sign said Belzec. It was the train station. I knew that sinister brick building held secrets. We stared at each other for a moment, but didn't speak. Then down the road a few hundred yards, beyond a long wall with an open gate, the landscape to my left sloped upward, away from me. It looked like the moon. This was it.

I pulled into a dirt lot, and we bumped over the potholes toward the other cars that didn't want to be there either. There was no ticket taker, no ticket seller, no directions, and no instructions. I was alone. How could I be in a place where half a million people were murdered?

I got out of the car. David walked directly to the memorial. An ear-piercing screech hit. It was a railroad whistle. Evidently all the tracks hadn't been torn up. Another train was arriving at the camp. Who could have arranged such a horrible joke? Within the biting sound of the whistle I heard the wheels of time, grinding and rattling, speeding past on metal rails. Tears ran down my checks.

I opened the back of the car to get my jacket and my hat. I needed to be covered up even though the summer sun was beating down. In my knapsack I found the paper with the names of Chana Becker's kin. She was the email contact who had lost family at Belzec and asked me to look them up. I stuffed the names into my pocket, found a tissue and dried my eyes. I went behind the low wall of the memorial and lost my breath.

The memorial was a moonscape of black and gray pumice stone strewn across acres of the former camp. Rusted and twisted iron poles stuck up from the ground. A rectangle of narrow sidewalk, fifty or sixty yards on a side, bordered this other planet. The names of each town that had unwillingly contributed victims to this place thrust themselves onto the sidewalk in rusted names, letters twisted once in English and once in Hebrew. There were hundreds of names. Do you hear me? There were hundreds of names of cities and towns who lost their breathing, laughing, living souls to this monster.

For what reason?

Round manholes every few hundred feet couldn't hold the stench of death beneath the ground, the smell of hundreds of thousands of decomposing bodies. "Grandmother, that stink that rises from the open grates in the ground, I know what it is."

To create the border of the memorial, the camp was arbitrarily fenced. In a far corner lay the tank traps that were dug by the inmates during WWII under orders from their nazi captors, to keep the Russian army from advancing from Ukraine.

In another corner of the memorial lay a kind of modern sculpture, or was it just a stack of railroad ties? Nearby sat a teenager, a member of an Israeli tour group. He was playing Israeli music on a boom box. The music was loud, but it didn't carry across the acres of open space. It reminded me I had made a good decision not to bring my clarinet to Belzec.

I wanted to be invisible. I wore a coat and a hat in the summer heat. I had grown a beard. I wanted to be an anonymous Jew in Poland. I needed protection. I didn't want to be identified. I didn't look anyone in the eye. I was careful, very careful with my footsteps.

I approached a passageway, a tunnel with no roof, dug between two sections of the memorial. The passage ran from the entrance to a wall at the back of the camp.

The wall was inscribed with victims' names. But the pathway to the wall of names was roped-off for repairs. I couldn't get there to see if my family was remembered. I couldn't see about Chana Becker's names. But I was relieved I wouldn't have to walk through the cemetery on a path dug between the bones and bodies and ashes. I was content to remain above them. I wondered how such a thing could have been done; a path dug through a cemetery the way a child would dig in the sand at the beach.

I cried. As I walked around the border of stones, I talked to my grandmother. I ripped a sheet of paper from my notebook and wrote a note. "Dear Grandmother: I came to see you and Uncle Yantsche and Uncle Meyer."

I wanted her to know that I had come, that I remembered her. I wanted to give her the note. I was standing on the concrete border and knelt down, so I could reach the gray stones. I looked around to see if anyone was watching because I felt silly writing a note to a dead person. There was no one in sight. I stooped to the ground and hid the note under a stone. I got up and walked around the sidewalk bordering this other planet, a field of stones from which trees sprouted. How could trees grow from rocks? I did not know. Silence was everywhere. I hummed a klezmer tune that came into my head—the "Heyser Bulgar." For a moment, it rescued me from this nightmare of a place and connected me to something familiar. It stopped me from crying.

Then I thought that I should leave a note for my grandmother beside the rusted words of Gorlice, her home. I was trying to put a logical idea into a completely illogical place. Did it make sense? Who can say? Regardless, I walked to the "Gorlice" name around the other side of the memorial and wrote another note, this one from me and all my cousins, Malka's grandchildren. I included all of their names. "Grandmother, we are thinking of you," the note said. I folded it and anchored it under a stone near the Gorlice marker. How silly that I didn't think to include my father's name in the message.

A one-story building held a museum. Exhibits detailed the camp with pictures of the inmates and old maps of the killing places. I examined every picture, hoping to see a photo of my grandmother or some other crumb of evidence that she lived. I listened to a movie describe how the inmates were fooled and cajoled into getting on the train to Belzec. They were told they were being resettled. The voice in the movie said one group of inmates was happy to have been promised work by the commandant of the camp when they lined up in orderly fashion to hear him speak shortly after arriving. It seemed as if they didn't perceive their fate, or believe what their eyes were seeing, until they were marched into a barracks where they crowded onto eight benches and were met by eight Jewish barbers who shaved their heads. Only then did they understand.

The land outside the fence also contained the burned and crushed bodies. How does one create a memorial to 500,000 people who didn't return home? There were no survivors, few telling witnesses. We know what to do to mark a birthday, but what is appropriate to mark this kind of place?

My cellphone vibrated. My son had sent me a text message. "Yanks lose 3 straight. In second place. A-Rod hit 600."

As if a rescuer had pulled me from the bottom of a chasm, I experienced the pleasure of waking from a nightmare.

I grabbed the lifeline and answered, "Who threw the pitch?"

Outside the fence, above the mass gravesite, was a dirt road. Three children played on a raised mound near the railroad tracks. I knew what lay under the mound. I strayed from the path into the high grass. For a moment I kicked into the dirt, but I didn't really want to find the fragments of bones that I knew lay not deep beneath the surface. It was time to go. But was there something else I had to do? Had I stayed long enough?

I had been scared to come here. I had thought about this journey for years and traveled thousands of miles, real and imaginary; I had to go see, but was very happy to leave.

I was leaving a Jewish cemetery and needed to wash my hands. I had never thought about the origin of this custom, but at that moment it was so clear that I needed to leave behind the spirits that clung to me, though I could have used a complete sanitizing, a purification of every molecule of my body and my clothing.

David was waiting for me in the parking lot. I returned my hat and jacket to the trunk and found a bottle of water in my knapsack that I poured over my hands. We silently got back into the car. I pulled out of the pot-holed dirt lot of Belzec and turned a corner. I didn't look back.

I wanted to get far away from that place as quickly as I could, but no car was fast enough to escape the racing memories. I needed a rocket or a time-machine – I couldn't break free. My seatbelt felt so confining, the inside of the car so small. I felt like stopping and screaming, or jumping, jumping, jumping or rolling over and over on the road. I didn't care. I was numb and on fire. I was enraged. I didn't know what to do or how to describe any better how I felt.

Perhaps an hour passed before David and I spoke. I don't remember who said the first word or what it was, but it had to be trivial and meaningless in comparison to what we had just experienced.

But I couldn't drive away from my history. Why would I want to? I had caught up with it, or it with me. Looking back, Belzec was a station on a journey that began when I was ten years old, when my father opened his secret suitcase and showed me that picture of my grandmother. It was then, more than forty years earlier, that I had begun my journey to claim my inheritance. My grandmother's letters fed what I can only describe as my mysterious responsibility to continue that journey.

Chapter 28

The Last Puzzle Piece

*A man watches a dancer perform. "What
does the dance mean?" he asks.
"If I knew, I wouldn't have had to dance
it," the dancer replies.*

I stood sleepily in the reentry line at JFK airport
with the long blue Customs Declaration form in my
hand. I carried no monetary instruments of $10,000 or
commercial merchandise. I carried no agricultural
products. There were no checkboxes on the form to des-
ignate one arriving with an inheritance, but I was
prepared to stand in the line under the sign that said,
"Items to Declare."

I was ready to declare my story.

With passport in hand I approached the young inspector's booth and handed over my papers. He looked me in the eye. I looked back.

"What was the purpose of your visit?" he said.

"I visited the house where my family lived more than seventy years ago."

"How was that for you?"

"Cool, very cool," I said.

I was tired, and I wanted to get home. I could have told the inspector about my journey, about the suitcase my father hid in his closet, about my grandmother's picture that made him cry and her letters written on onionskin paper. I could have told him about the history of the Jewish people wrapped up in the klezmer music that I played on the twenty-five-dollar clarinet my father bought for me in a pawnshop, or the prisoners I had seen while playing klezmer in the synagogue.

I didn't tell him about the sycamore tree that hid my father or about its seeds I wanted to plant in my garden. And I didn't tell him about my grandmother's name hammered into the shield that shines like gold in the sidewalk in front of her house in Leipzig, or standing under her window and playing a klezmer tune for her. I didn't tell him about the notes I left for my grandmother at Belzec.

I would have told him about the inheritance I carried, but he didn't ask.

He thumbed through the pages of my passport and gave it a brisk stamp with the metal plunger on his desk.

"Welcome home," he said.

After some weeks at home, I noticed that something

about my father's suitcase was different. It was ordinary, not as exciting as I remembered it had been when I was ten. I felt some separation from it. I didn't know why. And I had lost my taste to play klezmer clarinet for the first time in forty years. Again, I didn't know why. I felt a separation from my father's past even though it was also mine. I had thought he owned it, until I claimed my share. But I felt as if a piece of my puzzle was still missing.

One Sabbath morning, the rabbi made an announcement in synagogue. A group of yeshiva students were visiting from out of town. They were looking for study partners.

"These boys are future rabbis," he said. "Some of them will eventually lead their own congregations, but now they need more knowledge of Jewish communities—our customs, our habits, and our experiences."

Although I had turned down opportunities to study with similar groups who had come to visit over the years, this time something felt different. I didn't know exactly how I was going to do it, but I had an experience I wanted to share. And I was all for new teachers being able to practice their trade with study partners.

"Whatever they can glean will be helpful," the rabbi said from the podium.

I met up with him after the service, at Kiddush, somewhere between the tuna fish salad and the pickled herring.

"I'd like to do some studying. How about signing me up with one of the boys?"

He shook my hand. "Will do."

A few minutes later a young fellow, white shirt, black suit, twenty-something, stood in front of me. "I'm Joel Nathan," he said. "I hear you're interested in learning."

We made some small talk. He was from Far Rockaway, Brooklyn. Now he lived in Baltimore. We made an appointment for Monday at 9 a.m. in the synagogue.

I arrived at the appointed time, and he was waiting in the lobby. We shook hands. "What do you want to study?" he asked me.

"Oh, anything you'd like. You pick," I told him.

"Are you sure? There's nothing special you want to learn?"

"No. You can pick your favorite."

I knew His choice of topic would be significant. I didn't want to interfere.

Joel said, "I'll be right back," and returned in a moment with two chumashim, copies of the Old Testament. We sat at a table near the wall in the circular study room. He handed me a book and turned some pages. "Lech Lecha," he said, putting a finger on the Hebrew words that named the chapter. "Is that all right?"

I nodded half-heartedly because of the sudden lump in my throat. I wondered whether or not he could see it. Was it noticeable from the outside?

Joel read the first line of the chapter in Hebrew.

וַיֹּאמֶר יְהֹוָה אֶל־אַבְרָם לֶךְ־לְךָ מֵאַרְצְךָ וּמִמּוֹלַדְתְּךָ וּמִבֵּית אָבִיךָ

אֶל־הָאָרֶץ אֲשֶׁר אַרְאֶךָּ

He translated. "G-d said to Abram, go forth from your land and your birthplace and your father's house to the land I will show you." Then Joel asked, "Why did G-d tell Abram to do that? We can see that G-d doesn't even tell him where to go. He just says 'GO.'"

"Maybe G-d wanted to test Abram," I said.

"Maybe. Let's read some more."

After discussing the next sentence or two, Joel said, "The sages interpret this portion by saying that the words in the passage could be taken literally and figuratively. They could mean, Pick yourself up and leave physically, and they could mean, *Leave behind your unpleasant history and go forward. Go for yourself.*"

The lump in my throat got larger. I felt as if my fortune had just been told, or was it my past? My eyes began to tear. I don't remember much after that. I don't know if we talked any more, or even if I would have been able to talk. I only remember hearing the sound of the ocean in my ears. But at the end of the session, I thanked the young man and asked if we could study again, on Wednesday.

"Same time, nine o'clock?"

"See you then," I said.

I returned on Wednesday to the same desk. Joel was already seated. He pointed to the notebook in my hand. "What's in the book?" he asked.

"I have a story to tell you; it will take me five minutes. Okay?"

"I have as much time as you need."

I sat down and got comfortable in my chair. I had never told anyone the story I was about to tell. At that moment I wasn't sure how I'd shape it, but I jumped in.

"You know how sometimes you hear about people who find treasure in a trunk in the attic?" I said to him.

"Yeah, I've heard stories like that before, but I've never known anybody...Did you discover treasure in the attic?"

"Something like that happened to me. Some years ago, I found an old suitcase that my father had hidden for forty years at the bottom of his closet."

He squinted. "Forty years?"

"It was the suitcase my father carried when he fled on Kristallnacht from nazi Germany.

"Did you find out what was inside?"

"Stacks of letters bound up in old shoelaces."

"Letters? Who from?"

"My grandmother. During the war she wrote from Poland to my father in New York City. My father saved her letters."

He thought for a minute. He wanted to choose the right words. "Did she...?"

"Yes, she died in a concentration camp."

"Oh, I'm sorry," he said in a low voice; his eyes looked away.

"To make a very long story short, I ended up going to my father's house in Leipzig on the seventieth anniversary of Kristallnacht 1938, the day my father fled. I knew his address from the letters."

I leaned in towards him. "Joel, did you ever feel that you just had to do something but weren't quite sure why?"

He tilted his head toward the ceiling. "I don't know. Maybe, when I was little."

"Well, I had to go to my father's house on that day. I don't know why. I just had to. I felt like I was being pulled to a certain place, someplace I'd never been."

"So, did you go?"

"I did. I flew to Berlin and took a train to Leipzig. I went to my father's house. I'll tell you about that in a minute, but first let me tell you about my visit with a contact I made through a Jewish Genealogical Club. It turned out that she was the secretary of a synagogue, which happened to be the only synagogue out of twelve to survive the arson of Kristallnacht in 1938."

Joel pulled his chair closer.

"In her office, she handed me an envelope. 'Look inside, it's for you,' she said. When I opened the envelope, I found the membership cards of my father, my grandmother, and an aunt and uncle, all dated 1935."

"That's unbelievable. And you didn't know?"

"My father never talked about it. That's why I had to go see for myself."

"That's unbelievable," he said again.

"If it didn't happen to me, I wouldn't have believed it either. The next day was Saturday, and I went to services. I was called to the Torah. Want to guess what the portion was?"

I could hear the wheels turning in his head.

"Lech Lecha. It was Lech Lecha," I said. Joel's mouth, which had been hanging open, formed into a wide grin.

"I'm going to show you a note in my journal that I made on November 10, 2008, when I was in Leipzig. I want to show you, so you don't think I'm crazy or that I made this stuff up." I fanned through the pages of my notebook until I came to the place. I put the book between us and pointed to the words.

> *I traveled more than 3,000 miles to come to my father's house. I am called to the Torah in front of the whole community, in the same synagogue where my father was Bar Mitzvah. I could feel his presence in the room. We heard the words of G-d in the parsha. 'Get thee out of your father's house.' Just the opposite of what I want to do. So confusing."*

"I remember feeling embarrassed when I was in Germany and wondered if I had done the wrong thing to come to Leipzig, to my father's house. I couldn't make sense of it. It was a trip that had been bottled up inside me since the first time I had seen my father's suitcase."

My voice was cracking, and I had to pause. I stood up and stretched. I cleared my throat.

"But you explained it all to me on Monday," I said to Joel. "You told me what it was all about. Remember when you said the words could be interpreted to mean: '*Leave behind your unpleasant history and go forward for yourself*'?" I closed my notebook and we both leaned back in our chairs. I don't remember what we said afterwards, maybe because my story was still hanging in the air; I could hear it as I thought about my father's suitcase and where it had taken me.

I don't believe in coincidences, and I wasn't about to begin. I didn't ask Joel why he had picked that chapter to study. I did not want to know.

Epilogue

The first time I tried to write the story of the letters, the story of my father's secret suitcase, I attempted to concoct a novel. I invented characters. I told the story in the third person. I couldn't use real names. When I wrote my father's name, the ink in my pen froze. I was embarrassed to tell my story, which I didn't want to claim as my own. I wasn't ready for my inheritance.

If I had never possessed the suitcase, and if it had never possessed me, things would have been different. I never would have understood how my father could have left his mother and Lola in Europe, while he fled to safety. I might never have forgiven him for that. A part of me would have been stuck, not knowing my story, not being able to tell my story, stuck with filling up a suitcase with tales of my own invention. A childlike proposition, an adult not knowing where he came from, and not knowing how to get back home again. But I had to see for myself. I went to a place I feared.

I don't begrudge my father's approach to his handling of our history, only that I had to wait until after he died to re-release the story in my own handwriting. I had to wait until there was no one defending and deflecting before I could enter the story on my own terms.

My journey came in puzzle pieces, which I arranged into a picture that fit neatly onto my kitchen table. I had garnered those puzzle pieces from teary stories and distilled them from letters written on onionskin paper. I had witnessed them in my parents' sighs and stares. They came from the aroma of musty paper, a familiar sepia smile, the snap of unlocking clasps, a shadow on a suitcase. The pieces were cut from pictures old and new.

I fixed those scattered bits together with the history in a klezmer melody, with the excitement in a ten-year-old boy's imagination, and with memory's glue. I made a canvas, a portrait that looked as if it had always been.

It is my picture. It is me.

"Who knows only his generation remains always a child."
— Cicero

What They Said

"Dear Max, if you can go, and if you must go, please don't stay because of me, you could miss the ship... So, I wish you much happiness for your trip..." (Malka, November 6, 1938)

"I don't know whether I can come home anymore." (Malka, November 6, 1938)

"Everyone became poor in an hour." (Malka, November 11, 1938)

"Unfortunately everywhere there is misery." (Malka, March 26, 1939)

"Lola will also be glad that I have a nice apartment... the kitchen is also nice and betampte." (Malka, January 11, 1939)

"I would like to see you married with dear Lola." (Malka, March 30, 1940)

"If your father carried those letters around for sixty years, he wanted you to have them. Go find out what they say." (Rabbi Friedman)

"Take these away. I never want to see these letters again." (Max)

"The history of our Jewish people is in that music."
(The author's mother, 1964)

"What will be with Max?" (Aunt Sidy, 1993)

"Your mother who loves you." (Malka, many times)

"We won. They lost." (Terri, 2003)

"I have to tell you. I am possessed." (The author)

"Do you know what happened here seventy years ago?"
(News reporter, Leipzig, 2008)

"You left your job to translate your grandmother's
letters." (A friend, 2003)

"It is fashionable to know Jews these days. We are
like the monkeys in the zoo." (Frau Krenn, 2008)

"How can Jews joke about such a thing?" (Inga, 2008)

"Peter Bein, the grandson of Malka Bein." (Adrienne,
the synagogue secretary, 2010)

"My grandmother left this earth without a trace."
(The author, 2009)

"Here lived Malka Bein." (Stolperstein, 2009)

"I'm with you." (The author's brother, 2009)

"You must separate the language from the crime."
(Frau Krenn)

"She was almost my mother." (The author)

"Grandmother, I know what that smell is." (The author)

"A-Rod hit 600." (Jacob, 2010)

"This tastes like my mother used to make." (Max)

"Maxl, if only one year from now we could be at Frau Bein's table eating her Passover cooking." (Lola, December 15, 1938)